CW01649254

LYRA MARTYRUM

LYRA MARTYRUM

THE POETRY OF THE ENGLISH MARTYRS, 1503–1681

Second Edition ꞉ *Expanded and Revised*

Edited and with an Introduction by
BENEDICT J. WHALEN

Originally compiled by THE REV. SIR JOHN R. O'CONNELL

Foreword by FRANCIS CARDINAL BOURNE

CLUNY MEDIA

Cluny Media edition, 2019

This Cluny edition is a revised and expanded republication of the edition originally published by Burns Oates and Washbourne, Ltd., in 1934.

For more information regarding this title
or any other Cluny Media publication,
please write to info@clunymedia.com, or to
Cluny Media, P.O. Box 1664, Providence, RI, 02901

VISIT US ONLINE AT WWW.CLUNYMEDIA.COM

Cluny Media second edition copyright © 2019 by Cluny Media LLC

All rights reserved

ISBN: 978-1950970537

NIHIL OBSTAT:
Eduardus J. Mahoney, S.Th.D., *Censor deputatus*

IMPRIMATUR:
Joseph Butt, *Vicarius generalis*
Westmonasterii, December 3, 1934

Cover design by Clarke & Clarke
Cover image: Bartolomeo Montagna, *Saint Justina of Padua*, 1490s, oil on wood
Courtesy of The Metropolitan Museum of Art, New York

CONTENTS

‡ APPENDIX ‡ 183

DEDICATED

to my beloved brethren,
the Fathers of the Catholic Missionary Society,
who are devoting their lives so zealously to win
back England to that Faith for which her
Martyrs died.

IN MEMORY OF RICHARD HARP

Joy of goodness, love of art,
Virtue wears him next her heart.

B. J. W.

FOREWORD

WE CANNOT KNOW TOO MUCH about the heroic men and women who gave their lives to save for England her ancient faith. Of some of them we know little but the bare story of their birth, their upbringing, some part of their missionary activity and their glorious martyrdom. Of a certain number we have a more complete knowledge from their letters or other writings which have been preserved to us. In this way we come to know more fully the spirit which filled them; the providential circumstances which guided their career; the persons, friendly or hostile, with whom they came in contact; the historic setting in which they moved. The fuller information that we are able to glean in this way, the more accurate is the picture that we are able to form for ourselves of their character, their influence and the place which they can claim in the history of the Catholic Church in this country.

Of a comparatively small number we are granted a deeper and more intimate perception, for God bestowed upon them, and they made use of, the gift of imaginative poetry to set forth the innermost thoughts of their souls. Did we not read the verses wrung from their hearts by the greatness of their love of God, or the extremity of their suffering, we should have only partial understanding of the significance of their lives. These poetical writings are not sufficiently known, partly because they could be found only scattered here and there.

Francis Cardinal Bourne
Archbishop of Westminster
Hare Street House
Feast of St. James, 1934

PREFACE

THE POEMS IN THIS ANTHOLOGY, now gathered together in as nearly as possible a complete form for the first time, are the expression of an aspect, a phase in one of the most amazing chapters in the history of the English people. Looking back upon that period from the distance of two centuries and a half, the revolt of England against the unity of the Catholic faith still continues to present problems which will probably never be satisfactorily explained. It is true that many causes combined to smooth the downward path of that great spiritual and moral declension. The widespread weakening of faith and devotion throughout Europe caused partly by the rivalries and warfare of nations and partly by the growth of secular learning, the increasing loss of spirituality and of fervor in many countries, the growth of antagonism to the Papacy throughout Germany and Central Europe, caused by the dissentions between the secular rulers and the Popes, the worldliness of some of the occupants of the Papal Throne and their political entanglements, created a situation throughout Europe which could not fail to have a disastrous effect on the stability of the Catholic Church in England. To these evil influences from

A NOTE ON THE TEXT: This Preface is the original introduction to the 1934 edition of *Lyra Martyrum*. It is retained in abbreviated form.

outside have to be added others not less serious from within. The worldliness and the political ambitions of the Papacy had found a counterpart in the ambition, the self-seeking and the ostentation of Henry VIII's mentor and greatest minister, Cardinal Wolsey, himself an unscrupulous candidate for the Papal Throne.

The evident worldliness and spiritual apathy of the Cardinal Legate could not fail to have a demoralizing effect on the outlook and the habits of many of the hierarchy and priesthood throughout the land. The rapidly-increasing moral decadence and immorality of Henry VIII, his ever-growing need for larger sums of money than could be legitimately raised by the ordinary methods of taxation and the gradual realization of the considerable accession of wealth which could be procured by the suppression and confiscation at the monasteries, the general confusion of mind of many of the clergy and of the laity as to the respective prerogatives and claims of the Pope and the King, the conflict between the spiritual authority and the temporal jurisdiction of Pope and King and the deplorable laxity of spiritual ideals and of religious observances in some, though by no means in all, of the monasteries, and, to a greater extent, in the parish life throughout the length and breadth of England; all these influences united to make easy the destruction of that church which had been the glory of England for over a thousand years. Other causes also tended to complete the separation of England from the unity of Christendom. The growth of the sense of nationality—the consciousness of an individual life in the nation—was fostered by the ambition of Henry VIII, and was helped in no small degree by that new body of his followers now rapidly arising in power and influence, men for the most part without family or tradition intent on making their way in the world at any cost by the sacrifice of any principle and who saw in the destruction of the monasteries and the plunder of the church a means of flattering their Sovereign, of satisfying his rapacious requirements, and of acquiring wealth for themselves. These and various other explanations have been advanced as the reasons why England—"the Dowry of Mary"—after a thousand years of faith and fervor within the sacred fold of the Catholic Church, broke away from the union of Christendom and renounced her allegiance to the Chair of Peter. In the light of all that has happened since that sad breach with the unify of the Catholic Church it may be said that the causes were twofold—the increasing growth of a national consciousness which tended to emphasize the individuality of the English nation and to separate it from the main current of European culture, and secondly the belief of Henry VIII and his advisers, that "the new forms of religion" would come to be accepted almost unconsciously by the majority of the people and that they would all become gradually welded into a national church deriving its authority from the state and dependent entirely on the Throne almost before they became conscious of any separation from the unity of the Catholic faith. That this was part of the definite policy of Henry VIII and his advisers is proved by the fact that they were careful to make but little change in the outward forms of worship and that, despite their destruction and spoliation of the monasteries, they made few changes in the outward practices of religion.

While Henry got the power and wealth of the Church into his hands he was content to let the people believe that no fundamental change had taken place in the essentials of their Catholic heritage. These schemes would have succeeded, and the people of England would almost imperceptibly and unconsciously have completely lost the Catholic faith if it had not been that almost from the beginning there were men and women of penetrating intellect, deep spirituality and dauntless courage who, fully realizing the efforts which were being made to rob the people of England of the heritage of their faith, took up a firm stand and opposed the new movement with determination and courage. Such at the very outset were the Blessed Thomas More and the Blessed Cardinal John Fisher. Inspired by their example there were, for more than one hundred and fifty years, heroic men, priests and laymen, and women who were prepared to sacrifice all that life holds dear and even life itself to preserve the faith and unity of the Catholic Church. From this conflict between the ambition, rapacity and wickedness of the King, backed up by the forces of Nationalism which he had called into play on the one part, and the faith and courage of those who were ready to sacrifice everything for their loyalty to the Church of God, there arose that long and bitter persecution, the story of which is one of the brightest chapters in the history of martyrdom for the faith and one of the darkest pages in the history of England.

For over one hundred and fifty years, from May, 1503, until July, 1681, some 360 men and women were put to death mostly by the revolting torture of hanging, drawing and quartering, throughout the length and breadth of the land. They suffered for no other reason except their devotion, loyalty and service to the Church of God. They were people of stainless lives, of unblemished reputation, virtuous, law-abiding, honest Christian citizens. Their one and only crime was their loyalty to the faith which their forefathers had cherished for many centuries; that they were faithful sons or daughters of the successor of Peter the Prince of the Apostles; or that they, being ordained priests of the Catholic Church, did minister as such unto the faithful, or that those faithful did succor and support and give shelter and protection to their pastors.

In this persecution was included every class and grade of the national life. Its victims included a Cardinal of the Holy Roman Catholic Church, a man who had held the highest office of the State as Lord Chancellor of England, two great and influential noblemen, the Earls of Arundel and Northumberland, over 220 priests, secular and regular, members of many of the Orders of the Church, Carthusians, Benedictines, Jesuits, Franciscans, laymen of every degree, high-born and humble, rich and poor, learned and unlettered, old and young. The persecution spared none who had the courage to withstand its tyranny and its terrors. As it took

Thomas More, the most learned man of his day, and the Blessed Thomas Abel and his two companions, the best theologians of the time, so it took Humphrey Pritchard, a Welsh serving man, Nicholas Horner, a tailor, William Pike, a joiner, Lawrence Bailey, a Lancashire yeoman, and Roger Wrenno, a Chorley weaver. Nor did it respect old age, for the Blessed Thomas Reynolds, O.S.B., was hanged, drawn and quartered at Tyburn in 1642, being then aged about eighty, and the Blessed John Lockwood suffered the same horrible torture at York in the same year, being then aged eighty-one, and the Blessed John Kemble (who will always be affectionately remembered as the original of the hospitable phrase "the Kemble pipe") suffered the same fate at Hereford in August, 1679, when he was well-nigh eighty, having discharged his sacred duties as a priest for fifty-four years. Nor did the enthusiasm or inexperience of youth shield either priest or layman. The Blessed James Bird was hanged, drawn and quartered at Winchester in 1593 at the age of nineteen. The Blessed Lawrence Humphrey, another layman, suffered the same fate at the same place at the age of twenty. The Blessed Thomas Felton, a Franciscan novice, the son of the heroic Blessed John Felton, was hanged at Isleworth in 1588 at the age of twenty, and the Blessed Robert Watkinson offered up his life at Tyburn on April 20, 1602, having been ordained priest only the previous month, at the age of twenty-three.

As this persecution showed mercy neither to rank nor learning, nor to the dignity of old age, or the generous self-sacrifice of youth, neither did it respect the dignity of womanhood, and so the Blessed Margaret Clitherow, refusing to plead, was killed by the horrible cruelty of being pressed to death at York in 1586, her crime being that she was a convert and receiver of priests, and the Blessed Margaret Ward was hanged at Tyburn in 1588 for rescuing a priest, and the Blessed Anne Line was hanged at Tyburn in 1601 for the crime of giving shelter to a priest.

Two famous historic incidents which occurred during this period of persecution were made the pretext to justify its continuance and its still more rigorous enforcement when other causes were tending to allay its violence. One was the insane and fanatical Gunpowder Plot of November 5, 1605, which was cleverly made use of to defend the enactment of severe penalties and to justify the further persecution of those who were described as "Popish Recusants." The other was the Titus Oates plot, the evil effects of which continued for several years and were only brought to an end with the shameful sentence of hanging, drawing and quartering carried out on the saintly Oliver Plunket, Archbishop of Armagh at Tyburn on July 11, 1681.

With the execution of the Blessed Oliver Plunket, the horrible practice of public execution for steadfastness in the Faith and loyalty to the Catholic Church and to the Supreme Pontiff came to an end, but the spirit which had devised and practiced it—the spirit of persecution, the hatred of the Catholic Church and of all that it taught and practiced—was far from abated. Although the public death penalty was no longer enforced, both priests and laymen in considerable numbers were still, on one pretext or another, kept in jail and in many cases died in prison from their sufferings and ill-treatment. For those of our faith who were not forced to endure the horrors of the prison house there long continued the daily trial of persecution in various forms—in the form of deprivation of civil rights, denial of opportunities of education and professional advancement, exclusion from opportunities of employment and preferment in all the more important avenues of occupation and of public service. Ostracism, professional, personal and social, continued to be the lot of the loyal Catholic for many generations. Persecution in this form was to continue for another century and a half until the Catholic Emancipation Act restored to the much tried members of the Catholic Faith most, though not all, of the rights of equal citizenship. Even now, more than a century after the enactment of Catholic Emancipation, can it be said that the old spirit of persecution, of unjust and unfair discrimination against the members of the older Faith, in certain aspects of the national life, especially in the matter of education, has entirely disappeared?

As has been said, the 360 men and women who, in the long persecution, between 1503 and 1681, gave their lives for the unity of the Catholic Church and for their loyalty to the Holy See, were drawn from different grades of society and were endowed with varying degrees of education and of intellect. A large number were men of considerable education and learning, graduates of the Universities of Oxford and Cambridge, the former University contributing the larger proportion. A few were members of one or other of the Inns of Court. The priests—many of whom were also graduates of one or other of these universities—completed their education as well as their ecclesiastical training in one of the English colleges abroad, at Douai, or Rheims, or Valladolid or Rome, and by their education, their training and their character they were well prepared to carry on their mission for the preservation and extension of the Catholic faith in their own country. By their zeal and their learning they were well fitted—as they proved themselves again and again when forced to hold controversy with members of "the new religion"—to defend the truths of Catholic teaching and to present its doctrines with convincing force and clearness. In one sense, perhaps, many of these martyr priests might be described as poets. If they did not write poetry they certainly lived poetry, for their entire lives were lived for the worship and service of God and to win souls for his greater glory. Poetry has been described as "the expression of the noblest emotion of the human spirit clothed in the noblest form of words," and in their lives of unceasing self-sacrifice for the attainment of the loftiest ideals these martyr priests are surely giving expression to "the noblest emotion of the human spirit" in their daily lives if not in words.

In this little anthology there has been gathered together as it is believed for the first time, as exhaustive a collection as has been possible of the English religious poems of the six martyrs who, in the century and a-half of active persecution, gave expression to their faith, their hopes and fears and sufferings in English verse. There were one or two others who left fragments of Latin or Gaelic poetry, but for obvious reasons it has not been considered worthwhile to include these fugitive pieces, and of those whose writings will be found in the following pages only those poems which are marked by a definitely religious character have been included, not only to keep this little book within reasonable limits, but still more because the religious poems of these writers are on a higher plane, both of inspiration and of execution than their secular writings. These six martyr poets, as in the case of their fellow sufferers, were drawn from widely different classes and belonged to different periods. The first, the Blessed Thomas More, some time Lord Chancellor of England, was one of the earliest victims of the fury of Henry VIII. Philip Howard, Earl of Arundel, born more than twenty years after More's beheading on Tower Hill, spent ten years in cruel imprisonment under sentence of death in the Tower of London, and died in 1595, more than a century after More was born. The Blessed Henry Walpole and the Blessed Robert Southwell, both members of notable families, both deeply imbued with the spirit of their age, both members of the Society of Jesus, were destined to bear testimony to their faith within a few months of each other in 1595. The Venerable Father John Thules, after a devoted life as a Missionary Priest in Lancashire, was hanged, drawn and quartered in Lancaster in 1616, while the Venerable Nicholas Postgate suffered the same terrible death at York after more than fifty years of unwearied labor as a priest in August, 1679, when the long period of more vindictive persecution was coming towards its close.

It is hardly necessary to say that the unity which is the aim of some anthologies, the union of time and of form, will not be found in this anthology. In the century and a-half which separates Nicholas Postgate from Thomas More the English language was undergoing a profound development. It was becoming more flexible, more adaptable to the needs of expression and the thoughts and ideals which called for utterance were themselves changing with the years. The England of the end of the reign of Charles II was as profoundly different, perhaps more profoundly different from the England which was horrified at the beheading of Thomas More, the greatest man of letters then living, in 1535, as the England of today is different from that which welcomed the accession of Queen Victoria. And yet, between all these poets it is believed—and this is, indeed, the reason and it is hoped, the excuse for this little volume—that the discerning reader will find a unity of a more subtle and yet of a more profound character, he will find that these martyr poets were, in very truth, preserving "the unity of the spirit in the bond of Faith," that all their work was united by that strongest link of unity which can only be forged by a common faith and in a common hope.

That most searching of all tests, the test of time, is proving the greatness of Sir Thomas More—the greatness of his learning, the greatness of his wisdom and the greatness of his sanctity. Four centuries, far from obscuring his fame have added to it, confirming that notable phrase used by the Emperor Charles the Fifth when the news of More's execution was brought to him that "for himself he would have preferred to lose the richest city of his Empire than such a subject." Within quite recent years much scholarly attention has been concentrated upon the English works, both in verse and prose, of Sir Thomas More, and scholars, on both sides of the Atlantic, have devoted much attention to his works, not only because of their intrinsic merits but also on account of the important place they occupy and the important influence they have exercised in the development of English literature both in poetry and in prose. Lord Campbell, in his *Lives of the Lord Chancellors,* writes "they will be found interesting not only on account of his extraordinary precocity, but as the exercises by which he became the earliest distinguished orator and the earliest elegant prose writer using the English language." This little anthology is only concerned with More's religious poetry, but it may not be out of place to point out that in the gradual growth and development of English literature, and especially of English prose, the influence of Thomas More's learning and humor, his flexibility of mind and his penetrating grasp of what was essential and what was unimportant, gave to his prose writings a vigor, an adaptability and a character which mark a distinct advance in the gradual development of English prose. It is only necessary to read the *Life of King Richard III,* written when More was one of the Under-Sheriffs of London, about the year 1513, to realize that More had gone a long way towards becoming the master of a very bright and subtle instrument.

When, twenty years after, he wrote *The Dialogue of Comfort against Tribulation,* and subsequently, when he wrote the letters from the Tower to his daughter Margaret Roper, it becomes evident that he had acquired a command of pure and virile English such as was hardly known in the generation prior to his own. From the standpoint of the development of literary form it may well be considered that the work in prose of More is of more significance than his poetry. As a poet, Thomas More would seem to be entirely directed and influenced by his strong and deep religious feeling. More did not write poetry because he loved poetry, but he wrote because he loved God and found in poetry a medium where with he could praise him. His whole life and his whole spirit were permeated by the desire to serve God and to live in unison with God, and he made use of poetry, just as he made use of the other qualities of his mind, to serve God. This feeling of the ever-present sense of the things of eternity finds perhaps its finest expression in the "Lamentation on the Death of Queen Elizabeth," written so early as 1503 on the death of Queen Elizabeth, wife of Henry VII and mother of Henry VIII. It is probably the finest "dirge" in English literature, with its insistent thunderous repetition closing each verse, "And lo, now here I lie."

Your selfe knows well that in this realme was I
Your queen but late, and lo, now here I lie.

The delicate humor which was one of More's most delightful qualities is manifested in "The Twelve Properties or Conditions of a Lover," in which the author describes the qualities rightly to be demanded from an ardent lover and then points the moral by showing how these qualities should be devoted to the love of the Master.

Serve God for love, then, not for hope of meed:
What service may so desirable be
As where all turneth to thine own speed?
Who is so good, so lovely eke as He
Who hath already done so much for thee,
As He that first thee made, and on the rood
Eft thee redeemed with his own precious blood?

Perhaps the finest example of More's poetic spirit is his translation of "A Prayer of Picus Mirandula unto God." Although the idea of this poem must be attributed to Pico della Mirandola yet More's translation and treatment is so free and so full of spirit that the poem may almost be regarded as his own. "The Godly Meditation" has been included—indeed, it would go hard to leave it out—although in form it can hardly claim a place among More's poems, but it is so much the expression of a noble courage and an unswerving faith, a rule of holy living and holy dying, that it could not justly be omitted from any selection of his works.

The Venerable Philip Howard, Earl of Arundel, was sentenced to death on a wholly unsustainable charge of treason in 1585, the unjust sentence was never executed, but he was kept a prisoner in the Tower of London for ten years until he died there on October 15, 1595. If, as has been suggested, his youth and early manhood were overshadowed by folly and vice, he made a noble reparation in ten years of cruel imprisonment, during which he lived the life of a saint and devoted himself, when not in prayer, to the writing and translation of books of devotion, including *Three Treatises on the excellence and utility of Virtue,* and a translation—afterwards frequently reproduced and reprinted—of the Venerable John Lanspergius' *Epistle in the person of Christ to the Faithful Soul.* The only poems which can with something approaching certainty be ascribed to the Venerable Philip Howard are given in the text. Of the poems of the Blessed Robert Southwell little need be said. They have won their way to an acknowledged and valued place in the noble edifice of English poetry. They have been a consolation and a joy for three hundred years to all those who love and value English religious poetry. The reason for this enduring affection for his poetry, and especially for his shorter poems, may be that Robert Southwell was endowed with the inspiration of a true poet. He, indeed, wrote poetry in an age when most gentlemen would aim at writing verse, but he wrote with a grace, a facility, a tender imagination and fancy, a curious originality of subject and of treatment which raised his work above that of any of the other martyr poets or, indeed, of most of his contemporaries; with a spirit which has won for him a place, secure and lasting, if not outstanding, in English literature. It may be of interest to suggest that in Southwell's poem the "Burning Babe" there is a curious and most significant anticipation—may one not call it almost a pre-vision vouchsafed to a martyr?—of the devotion to the Sacred Heart of Jesus, which was not to reach its full significance until nearly another century had passed, in the words:—

Yet none approach to warm their hearts or feel my fire but I,
My faultless breast the furnace is, the fuel wounding thorns;
Love is the fire, and sighs the smoke, the ashes shame and
scorns;

The fuel justice layeth on, and mercy blows the coals;
The metal in this furnace wrought are men's defiled souls;
For which, as now on fire I am to work them to their good;
So will I melt into a bath to wash them in my blood.

Attention may also be called to those two most beautiful poems: the paraphrase of Saint Thomas Aquinas' hymn "Lauda Sion Salvatorem" and the poem "Of the Blessed Sacrament of the Altar: The Christian Manna," but perhaps Southwell in the moments of his greatest spiritual and poetic inspiration never wrote anything finer than the poem "The Virgin Mary to Christ on the Cross," in which his Mother, apostrophizing her dying Son on the Cross, exclaims:

Jesus! my Love, my Son, my God, behold thy Mother washed
in tears;
Thy bloody wounds be made a rod to chasten these my
latter years"

—perhaps the most poignant lines in the whole of English religious poetry.

Of the poems of the Venerable John Thulis and the Venerable Nicholas Postgate:these were obviously inspired by the great spiritual earnestness and deep apostolic inspiration which supported them in the daily trials, disappointments and consolations of their arduous and ever-dangerous missionary toil. It may well be regretted that the circumstances of their lives were such that men capable of such inspiring and touching poetry were not able to give fuller expression to such remarkable gifts, but so far as is known—and every effort has been made in this direction—the poems now given for the first time in full in the text, traced in the British Museum manuscripts, are the only poems known to have been written by these Priest-martyrs. It is a touching tribute to the memory of the Venerable Nicholas Postgate who was hanged, drawn and quartered for the crime of Priesthood at York in 1679, at the age of 82, that his poem:

O Blessed God, O Savior sweet,
    O Jesus look on me!
O Christ, my King, refuse me not,
    Though late I come to Thee.

was the favorite hymn of the scattered and harried Catholics in the dales of Yorkshire for many generations after its venerable author had been called to a martyr's crown, and continued to be a source of strength and consolation to the Catholic people of the dales for many generations after he had passed away.

Rev. Sir John R. O'Connell

INTRODUCTION

THIS ANTHOLOGY of the poetry of the English martyrs was compiled by Rev. Sir John O'Connell and first published in 1934. In the volume's original introduction, retained in this edition as the Preface, O'Connell writes that the period covered here "is one of the brightest chapters in the history of martyrdom for the faith, and one of the darkest pages in the history of England." Writing when he did, Fr. O'Connell exhibits a particular confidence in the poets included in this volume, since none had as yet been formally canonized by the Catholic Church. Thomas More had been beatified by Pope Leo XIII in 1886, but he was not canonized until 1935. Not until 1970 did Pope Paul VI canonize the "Forty Martyrs of England and Wales," which included Philip Howard, Henry Walpole, and Robert Southwell. The other two poets in the anthology, John Thulis and Nicholas Postgate, were not beatified until 1987, when Pope St. John Paul II included them among the "Eighty-five Martyrs of England and Wales," and they are not yet canonized. Nevertheless, with this new edition of *Lyra Martyrum*, it is important to recognize that, in the eighty years since the anthology's original publication, every poet included here has been formally canonized or beatified by the Catholic Church.

Historical Context

The volume's original introduction provides a brief overview of the difficulties English Catholics endured under the government persecutions in the period of 1503–1681. The trials were indeed severe. When Henry VIII passed the Act of Supremacy in 1534 and declared himself the supreme head of the Church in England, English officials and clerics were obliged to affirm that act by oath. Those who refused to swear were fined, imprisoned, or (like Thomas More) executed. Persecution of Catholics continued under Henry's Protestant son, Edward VI, before ceasing under the rule of his Catholic daughter, Mary I, who reversed Henry VIII's impositions and realigned the English Church with Rome, turning her father's methods against dissenting Protestant clergy. Mary's reign, however, was brief, and she was followed by the Protestant Elizabeth I. Upon ascending the throne, Elizabeth reaffirmed her father's Act of Supremacy and then added her own Act of Uniformity in 1559. The Act of Uniformity required all Englishmen to attend weekly Anglican services, or suffer hefty fines and possible imprisonment. It heralded a universal persecution of English Catholics, affecting even commoners far from the cities and centers of power. Those who refused to attend Anglican services were said to have "recused" themselves; this gave rise to the term *recusant* as a label for English Catholics who would not assent to Elizabeth's claims of spiritual authority and would not attend the Protestant ceremonies. Pope Pius V's excommunication of Elizabeth in the 1570 papal bull *Regnans in excelsis*, and the Spanish Armada in 1588, provoked progressively more hostile and rigorous treatment of Catholics. Simply being a priest became a treasonable offense warranting execution, and even the act of attending a mass or sheltering a priest was considered treasonous, punishable by execution or life in prison.

One significant hardship English Catholics faced at this time was the lack of access to priests who could administer sacraments and give counsel. In response to this need, William Allen, an Englishman who had fled England after the Act of Uniformity, founded an English College in France, first in Douai and later in Reims, and another in Rome. His mission was to educate expatriate English Catholics for the priesthood, so that they could then return to England as missionaries to serve the isolated Catholics there. In the final thirty years of sixteenth century, more than six hundred brave priests would return to England in the face of grim danger; both John Thulis and Nicholas Postgate were among this number. At the same time, the relatively new but rapidly expanding Society of Jesus had also admitted many English Catholics fleeing Elizabeth's persecutions but longing to serve their suffering countrymen. Edmund Campion and Robert Persons arrived in England in 1580, the country's first two Jesuit missionaries. Within the next forty years, more than one hundred additional Jesuits followed suit.

Campion, who was canonized in 1970 as one of the "Forty Martyrs of England and Wales," had studied at Oxford University as a young man and his brilliance in public disputations had caught the attention of Queen Elizabeth. The early promise he had shown as a young Protestant made him doubly unwelcome upon his return to England as a Jesuit missionary. Campion and Persons regularly insisted, most notably in Campion's "Letter to the Council" (commonly called his "Brag"), that their mission had no political ends, that they were peaceful and honorable in their aims, and that they came only to minister to the faithful English Catholics who had no access to sacraments. Subsequent missionaries echoed this protest: theirs was not a political aim. Elizabeth's Privy Council, however, saw things differently, and worked diligently to spread tales of the rebellious, treasonous intentions of the secretive Jesuits. After a single year, Campion was caught, subjected to torture and interrogation, and then hauled out of prison for public disputations with Anglican divines. This proved an unwise tactic on the part of the English government, for although Campion was suffering from repeated turns upon the rack and unable to prepare for the disputations, he defended the Catholic position so well that he started to gain public sympathy, even among those not friendly to the Catholic religion. Elizabeth was desperate to make a positive example of Campion, even secretly offering to make him an archbishop, if only he would conform to the Church of England. Campion held firm, however, and Elizabeth's government ceased the disputations, convicted him of treason, and executed him by hanging, drawing, and quartering on December 1, 1581.

Campion's treatment became commonplace for captured Jesuits, other missionary priests, and even the lay Catholics. Hundreds were racked, interrogated about their contact with priests, or pressured to name others who attended mass or harbored priests. One common torture involved chaining the prisoner against a wall, so that only the very tips of the toes could touch the ground, and leaving the person there to suffer for hours. The effect of such a torture is markedly similar to that of crucifixion, not only putting terrible strains upon the limbs and joints, but also leading eventually to suffocation. Hanging, drawing, and quartering was a particularly monstrous practice, whereby the condemned was hung by the neck, but, just before losing consciousness, was cut loose and immediately placed upon a table and disemboweled as he lay dying. His organs were often tossed into a pot of boiling water, his heart lifted in front of the witnessing crowd, and his head cut off, to be placed on a spike above London Bridge or another prominent location. His body would then cut into four parts, with each part sent to the four points of the compass and displayed in some other part of the city or land. Nor were these tortures confined to men; Catholic women were subjected to them and other, more particular violations. Often, groups of priests and Catholics would be executed together, one by one, with those who came later being forced to witness the butchering of their companions.

Truly, then, was this "one of the brightest chapters in the history of martyrdom for the faith, and one of the darkest pages in the history of England." What is perhaps most remarkable is that, despite the brutality and fierceness of the persecutions, brave priests continued to return to England, and continued to be welcomed by the brave, enduring faithful. Less remarkable, but still of singular importance, is the fact that in the midst of these desperate circumstances, some of those on the road to martyrdom turned to poetry. With their devotional verse, these martyrs took part in a much brighter page of English history: its literary tradition.

Literary Context

George Herbert, who figures prominently in the flowering of English devotional poetry in the seventeenth century, sent two sonnets to his mother while studying at Cambridge University. In the letter containing the sonnets, Herbert declares, "My poor abilities in poetry shall be all and ever consecrated to God's glory."[1] The first sonnet, some of Herbert's earliest surviving poetry, questions the typical subject of lyric poetry:

> My God, where is that ancient heat towards thee,
>   Wherewith whole shoals of martyrs once did burn,
> Besides their other flames? Doth Poetry
>   Wear Venus' livery? only serve her turn?

Only seventeen years of age, Herbert resolves to redirect poetry from earthly loves associated with Venus to divine subjects—a resolution he followed to remarkable effect throughout his life. This sentiment was not, however, without precedent in Renaissance England. Indeed, although the Anglican Herbert likely did not have him in mind when he wrote these verses, Robert Southwell (executed fifteen years before Herbert's letter), expressed similar

1. George Herbert, *The Complete English Works*, ed. and intro. Ann Pasternak Slater (New York: Everyman's Library, 1995), p. 344.

reflections about poetry and its proper ends. In a prefatory letter that accompanied the initial 1595 publication of Southwell's longer poem, *Saint Peter's Complaint*, he wrote, "Poets, by abusing their talent, and making the follies and feignings of love the customary subject of their base endeavors, have so discredited this faculty that a poet, a lover, and a liar are by many reckoned but three words of one signification."[2] On the same note, Southwell resolves in his prefatory lyric "To the Reader":

Prophane concietes and fayning fits I flie,
Such lawless stuffe doth lawless speeches fit:
With *David* verse to virtue I apply,
Whose measure best with measured wordes doth sit.

It is likely that George Herbert read Robert Southwell's poetry, as it was frequently republished, and was quite popular among English Catholics and Protestants alike (the latter owing to the purging of offensive Catholic references by Protestant printers). Furthermore, scholars have demonstrated ways in which Herbert's poetry shows Southwell's influence. So while Herbert's question "Doth Poetry / Wear Venus' livery? only serve her turn?" is certainly meant to be rhetorical, he was to learn, if he did not already know, of one great poet who had already decked poetry in the livery of a very different divinity.

This brief example illustrates that, while none of the poets featured in this volume are common household names, or even regarded as central figures of the golden age of English religious verse, without exception they either directly influenced

2. See p. 185, below. Several scholars have noted that William Shakespeare seems to be aware of Southwell's criticism of contemporary poetry, and that he responds to Southwell within his plays. For a good example, see Donald Carlson's "Of Lunatics, Lovers, and Poets: The Conversation about Poetry in Shakespeare's *A Midsummer Night's Dream*," *The Ben Jonson Journal*, Vol. 25, No. 2 (2018): pp. 194–213.

the religious turn in seventeenth-century English poetry or are themselves notable examples of that development. This historical period saw the composition of many of the most significant devotional works in the entire history of English literature. Among the great Protestant contributions to the literary tradition is John Bunyan's prose *Pilgrims Progress*, and in verse, Edmund Spenser's *The Faerie Queene* and John Milton's *Paradise Lost*. George Herbert's *The Temple* contains individual lyrics of great poetic and spiritual value, and the collection as a whole comprises one of our tradition's finest poetic explorations of the soul, and the joys and sufferings of the spiritual life. Mary Sydney's verse translations of the Psalms, John Donne's "Holy Sonnets", and, of course, various beautiful English translations of the Bible, including the King James Version, all are composed and widely read in this period.

Catholics, too, turned to poetry as a means for further religious expression, meditation, and prayer. Thomas More, for example, writes several poems that work within an established tradition that reaches back to Boethius's *Consolation of Philosophy*. Boethius famously portrayed Fortune as a woman turning a wheel, a figure of the fickle, ever-changing fortunes of men. More's early poems—see "To Them That Trust in Fortune" (p. 15) and "To Them That Seek Fortune" (p. 21)—emphasize the uncertainty of fortune and the likelihood of loss and suffering in life, themes which recur in More's prose writings and reemerge with pointed force in the poems that he composed while imprisoned and facing execution. Later religious poets in the English Renaissance also work within this tradition, including John Milton and John Donne. So too does Robert Southwell, in "Fortunes Falsehood" and "From Fortunes Reach." Themes or motifs like this are commonly shared by the poets included within this anthology and the larger community of English devotional poets. As another prominent example, Robert Southwell is notable for having written so much poetry focused upon tears. In writing about the tears of the Virgin Mary, of St. Peter, and of Mary Magdalene, Southwell played an influential role in developing what became the popular motif of "tear poetry" and "tear literature" in seventeenth-century religious verse. Shakespeare, Herbert, Crashaw, and Marvell all write within this tradition following Southwell's popular poems. Finally, the composition of hymns was both widespread and significant as a popular means of teaching and expressing articles of faith and important points of tradition. The poems included here by John Thulis and Nicholas Postgate can be read within this tradition of hymns, expressing both penitence and confidence in God's mercy and Christ's resurrection.

Poetry and Martyrdom

Yet the poems in this anthology share a more distinctive trait: They were composed by men who died for the Catholic faith. The following question, then, naturally presents itself: What has martyrdom to do with poetry, or poetry with martyrdom? Certainly, in these poems we find great conviction about the truths of the Catholic religion, the errors of Protestant reformers, and the poets' own resolutions to be steadfast in their faith. But none of this is necessarily or exclusively to be found in the poetry of martyrs. Similarly, some of these poems were clearly composed as devotional practices, as the very means of performing a meditation or uttering a heartfelt prayer. Thomas More's "The Twelve Weapons of Spiritual Battle" (p. 31), for instance, develops and explores a series of propositions; he moves from meditations on the passing and trivial nature of earthly pleasures, to the reality of judgment and eternal reward or punishment, and, finally, to the example of the total sacrifice of Christ and his martyrs. Their profundity notwithstanding, these meditations are not particularly shaped or informed by More's own impending martyrdom, and some of them are commonplaces within the larger traditions of Christian mediation. So too, some of these poems are intended to instruct and exhort the reader. This turn to teaching and exhortation is usually driven by manifestly charitable intentions. For example, John Thulis concludes his exhortative "Song of a Happy Rising" by addressing himself to his reader as "your friend," and demonstrating his charitable sense of Christian brotherhood in praying that God will "us all to heaven send." Similarly, Walpole's "A Dialogue Between a Catholic and Consolation" is meant to both console and strengthen the commitment of his Catholic readers. Yet these charitable elements can hardly be said to be exclusive to the poetry of martyrs.

There are, however, a few characteristics that seem more precisely to spring from the fact that most of these poems were written by men who even at the moment of composition faced mortal danger on account of their faith. Unsurprisingly, then, among the most significant of these common features is the prominence of death as a theme and subject. For example, in Philip Howard's "A Fourfold Meditation" (p. 63), death takes its traditional place as one of the four last things—death, judgement, heaven, and hell. When Howard composed the poem, he was imprisoned and already sentenced to death, yet doomed to live for years with the uncertainty of which particular day would bring the execution of his sentence. Howard could appreciate how this did, in fact, mirror the uncertainty that looms behind all human life, but his continual confrontation with expected and then delayed execution contributes a certain urgency to his reflections upon the four last things. When he addresses himself, "Thou art not sure one moment for to live" (ln. 7) and stresses that to "live thou must a thousand deaths to die, / and dying still, yet never wholly dead" (ln. 115–16), we can hear the particular difficulties of his daily experience. The struggle with death simply becomes the present: "The time will come when Death will thee assault: / Conceive it then as present for to be" (ln. 13–14), and this resolution to live as one dying allows him to proceed in the poem to fruitful penitence and then hopeful dependence upon God's mercy. In Robert Southwell's "I Die Alive" (p. 142), we find a meditation similar to

Howard's, as Southwell reflects upon the transience of life. But for Southwell, *Christ's* death becomes the more common subject for his poetry. His poems examine Christ's death from various perspectives, as we see in "The Virgin Mary to Christ on the Cross" (p. 135) and "Mary Magdalen's Complaint at Christ's Death" (p. 136). In these poems, Southwell develops a rich context for contemplating Christ's sacrifice—it is not only the mysterious act in which the all-powerful Son of God offers Himself up to redeem mankind, but also the particular, individual tragic event in which this good mother watches her Son slowly die, or in which this loyal disciple is racked by sorrows as she loses her beloved friend and leader. These instances demonstrate that these poets pondered death both as an imminent threat to themselves and as a reality that Christ before them had suffered, manifesting the perfection of sacrificial love, a sacrificial love that these martyrs too would ultimately exhibit.

Another repeated refrain in the poetry of this volume is the poet's need for consolation in the face of impending tortures, false accusations, and executions. Robert Southwell, for instance, had seen many of his students and friends led to suffer agonizing deaths. The need for consolation and fortitude in this context was not an abstract, intellectual question for him, nor was it simply a matter of theological or spiritual conviction. The horrors and tortures he and his fellows faced were such from which the flesh naturally shrinks. Thus, while other devotional poetry from the period seeks consolation or expresses real spiritual difficulties for the poet, repeatedly in the poems collected here, the urgency of the poet's situation, and the reality of the physical terrors soon to be inflicted upon him (or in some cases, which he has already in part endured), impart a decided influence upon the tone and sentiment in the poetry. To take one example, Henry Walpole witnessed Edmund Campion's death, being close enough to him as he was disemboweled to be splattered with Campion's blood, and immediately following the execution he converted to

Catholicism and headed to the continent for a Catholic education and eventual ordination. His poem "Upon the Death of M. Edmund Campion" focuses upon Campion's severed head and "quartered limbs." Walpole writes,

> We can not fear a mortal torment, we,
> This Martyr's blood hath moistened all our hearts,
> Whose parted quarters when we chance to see,
> We learn to play the constant Christian's parts.
> His head doth speak, and heavenly precepts give,
> How we that look should frame our selves to live.

Here Walpole repeatedly affirms that different physical parts of Campion's body strengthen and confirm the spiritual lives of those who witnessed his dismemberment. This transition from the physical to the spiritual is mirrored by Walpole's striking use of a type of pun, *antanaclasis* (in which a word is repeated but with a different meaning), when the "*parted* quarters" of Campion's body teach his audience their "Christian *parts*." Campion's body, even as it is being mutilated, becomes the exemplary model for the faithful Christian. Thus, the terrors of torture and execution are transfigured in Campion's example, and this inspires and consoles Walpole, and by extension, his readers. Walpole's poem is carefully crafted, but his purpose here is not literary artifice alone, nor simply an exhibition of his poetic ability. The need for consolation and a firming of the will is real, and has immediate consequences for Walpole. He not only converted to Catholicism and sought ordination on the continent, but fourteen years after witnessing Campion's execution, Walpole would suffer the same brutal end.

Finally, and perhaps most significantly, the poems collected here are distinctive as the work of martyrs because, although they temporally preceded the execution of each martyr, each poem is the fruit of the spiritual and intellectual lives of these poets, and so too is each martyrdom. The poems are artful expressions of prayer and thought, creations that arise from the intense, fruitful inner lives of these men determined to serve God. Their martyrdoms too are the fruit, the final fruit, of the lives of prayer and thought that directed these men's actions. Their poetry, then, is itself a kindred fruit to the poet's future embrace of martyrdom; both spring from the poet's faith and the active grace that moved him. Martyrdom is, among other things, an act of generosity on the martyr's part; having been given life, he gives it back, a magnanimous action which, while incomparably insignificant with respect to the greatness and efficacy of Christ's sacrifice on the cross, nevertheless is of a kind with it. Thus, just as Christ sang a hymn after the Last Supper, before heading to his torments, so too do these martyrs sing, pouring out their poems in preparation for the greater act of pouring out their blood for Christ.

Benedict J. Whalen, Ph.D.
Hillsdale, Michigan
Presentation of the Blessed Virgin Mary, 2019

SAINT THOMAS MORE

(1478–JULY 6, 1535)

THOMAS MORE WAS FAMOUS throughout Europe for his learning, legal and political brilliance, and vigorous defense of the Catholic Church. His execution in 1535 was one of the earliest, and most infamous, martyrdoms to result from the English Reformation. Indeed, in the years following his death, three separate biographies of More circulated in England despite the government's attempts to suppress them, and accounts of his life and death were published throughout Europe. Catholics immediately regarded him as a martyr, and many were to follow his courageous example as the persecutions escalated.

More was born in February 1478 to a wealthy family. His father, Sir John More, pursued a thriving career in law, eventually rising to the prestigious position of judge on the King's Bench. Thomas was provided with an excellent formal education, studying at the best grammar school in London and eventually at Oxford University. He was also given an excellent practical education; at the age of twelve, he was placed in the household of Archbishop Morton, who at that time was Lord Chancellor of England, and who was continually dealing with people and affairs of the greatest importance. Even in this courtly, refined setting, the young More stood out. One famous story tells of him suddenly stepping in and performing an impromptu part in a set of

Christmas revels performed for the Archbishop's house. His performance so impressed the Archbishop that he said More would prove to be a "marvelous man," and he placed him as one of his particular protégés at Oxford. Unafraid of public pressure, and brilliant in his mastery of language, More went on to study law, and quickly encountered great success. His steady rise involved admission to the King's Council in 1518, and culminated in his appointment as Lord Chancellor of England in 1529.

While More was achieving such exceptional professional success, he was also producing scholarship that made him famous throughout Europe. He was the close personal friend of Erasmus, among other leading humanists, and he wrote biographies and histories, philosophical dialogues, and theological works that addressed many of the most pressing issues of the day. He is best known today for *Utopia*, a witty and learned book that both satirizes aspects of contemporary Europe and engages in serious philosophical debates about the nature and ends of law, the relationship between the individual and the political community, and the place and duties of learned men with respect to those in power. More wrote widely about education, rhetoric, and the relation between learning and Christian wisdom and holiness. Several of the poems included in this volume are excerpted from larger works addressed to these subjects. More's attention was also much occupied, especially in his later years, with Protestantism. Perhaps the most important work he produced in this vein is his *Dialogue Concerning Heresies*, published shortly before he became Lord Chancellor, which offers a forceful, careful, and at times humorous defense of the Catholic Church, attacking Lutheran arguments, rejecting *sola scriptura* as historically incoherent, defending tradition and the clergy, and offering criticisms and correctives for corruption within the Church.

More's personal life is no less remarkable than his professional and scholarly accomplishments. As a young man, he spent a good deal of time with the Carthusians in London, and though he married and raised a family, he continued to embrace a life of prayer, study, and mortification. Yet, despite these points of simplicity and devotion, More was famous in his own day for his good cheer and ready wit. He was such delightful company that Henry VIII often desired him to spend the evenings with the King and Queen to entertain them with his conversation. His house was constantly busied with guests, and he gained such a reputation for taking care of the poor that he had to build a separate house on his grounds where the constant influx of needy might be adequately cared for without crippling the other operations of his household.

More had a close and loving relationship with his family, overseeing his children's education, and insisting that education was just as important for his daughters as for his son. Correspondence between More and his children shows his gentle but principled approach to his children, and how much he was admired by them. His letter to his children's teacher similarly reveals his deep concerns about the pride and vanity that often accompany intellectual achievements. Humble modesty, rather than pride in accomplishments, must be encouraged by the proper teacher. Indeed, More sought to educate and cultivate a virtuous disposition in all entrusted to him. As just one example, More's daughter-in-law kept asking him for a necklace with pearls set in it. More tried to redirect her desires many times, but finally, when she asked once more, he pulled out a box and solemnly gave it to her. She was delighted, and opened it to find that there was indeed a necklace, but set with white peas instead of pearls. Chastened by this lesson, we are told that she never afterwards desired new ornaments, although as More's biographer Gerard Wegemer notes, "The final part of this story is that Anne's portrait shows her wearing a pearl necklace, undoubtedly a gift from her wise and generous father-in-law."[1]

1. Gerard B. Wegemer, *Thomas More: A Portrait of Courage* (Princeton, NJ: Scepter Publishers, 1995), p. 83.

When Henry VIII first sought a divorce from Catherine of Aragon, Thomas More was on the King's Council, but refused to participate in the Council's efforts to gain the Pope's approval. Leaving it all to Cardinal Wolsey, More had focused upon different affairs of the state (mainly legal reforms and the correction of heresies). When Wolsey was deposed for failing to secure Rome's approval, however, More's elevation to Lord Chancellor put him in an awkward position. He had made it clear to the King he would not help him with this attempt at divorce, although he also did not openly state his reasons or objections. Things quickly deteriorated: Henry VIII, disappointed with Rome's refusal to recognize his divorce, decided to reject Roman jurisdiction and papal authority in England. More could not approve of this path either, and when Henry VIII declared himself Head of the Church of England, More did what he could to encourage the clergy to assert independence from the state, and then resigned the chancellorship in May of 1532. Despite More's attempts to withdraw from political affairs, his silence was widely understood as disapproval. In 1533, he refused to attend Anne Boleyn's coronation, and in 1534, the angered King insisted that More break his silence and swear to the Act of Succession, which had a preamble rejecting papal authority. When More refused, he was imprisoned in the Tower of London on April 17, 1534.

Thomas More spent the last fifteen months of his life in the Tower, where he faced tremendous pressure to submit, including deeply painful disagreements with his family. He was steadfast, however, and passed these final months composing his last works, the *Dialogue of Comfort* and *The Sadness of Christ*. In both of these, More finds his example and comfort in Christ, and reconciles himself to his impending death. They are sober, powerful meditations, the latter of which has survived in manuscript. More was brought to trial in July 1535; among the judges presiding over the trial were Thomas Boleyn and George Boleyn, Anne's father and brother. The outcome of the trial was never in question. The only real evidence presented against him was an account by Richard Rich, the solicitor general, who claimed that More had spoken against the King's new title in his presence. There were two other supposed witnesses to this treasonable conversation—at the time they had been present in More's cell to confiscate his books—but both notably refused to corroborate Rich's account. One of these witnesses was Richard Southwell, the grandfather of the poet and martyr Robert Southwell (included in this volume). Although Richard Southwell had accepted the King's claims to be Head of the Church of England, and although he was profiting from the pillaging of the monasteries, he offered up the transparently absurd excuse that "because he was appointed only to look to the conveyance of his books, he gave no ear" to what was said.[2] It was clear that Rich's testimony was false, and that Southwell refused to perjure himself or betray More. Nevertheless, the jury found More guilty. When More's verdict was given and he was sentenced to death, he abandoned his course of silence, and spoke powerfully against the King's claim to be head of the Church of England. He made such a case that the judges paused, and the Chancellor refused to have the judgement rest upon himself, depending upon other judges to make ambiguous qualifications in order to undermine More's argument and justify his sentence. While the normal execution for a traitor was hanging, drawing, and quartering, Henry VIII commuted the sentence to simple beheading.

Accounts of More's death are much like accounts of his life: measured and prayerful, but also full of good cheer and wit. As More was climbing the scaffold, he famously commented, "I pray you, Master Lieutenant, see me safe up, and for my coming down let me shift for myself."[3] Similarly, he exchanged forgiveness with

2. William Roper, *The Life of Sir Thomas More, c. 1556*, ed. Gerald B. Wegemer and Stephen W. Smith (Irving, TX: Center for Thomas More Studies, 2003), p. 52.
3. Ibid., p. 58.

his executioner, even cheerfully embracing him. More's body was buried in an unmarked grave, and his head, after having been displayed on a pike above London Bridge for some time, was rescued by his daughter Margaret, and is likely buried with her in St. Dunstan's, Canterbury.

Sources and Further Reading:

Bolt, Robert. *A Man for All Seasons*. New York: Random House, 1990.

House, Seymore Baker. "More, Sir Thomas [St. Thomas More] (1478–1535)." In *Oxford Dictionary of National Biography*. New York: Oxford University Press, 2004.

More, Thomas. *The Essential Works of Thomas More*. Edited by Gerard B. Wegemer and Stephen W. Smith. New Haven, CT: Yale University Press, 2020. http://www.essentialmore.org/

Roper, William. *The Life of Sir Thomas More, c. 1556*. Edited by Gerald B. Wegemer and Stephen W. Smith. Irving, TX: Center for Thomas More Studies, 2003. https://www.thomasmorestudies.org/docs/Roper.pdf

Wegemer, Gerard B. *Thomas More: A Portrait of Courage*. Princeton, NJ: Scepter Publishers, 1995.

The Poetry of Saint Thomas More

‡ ‡ ‡

The Ages of Man

CHILDHOOD

I am called Childhood, in play is all my mind,
To cast a quoit,[4] a cockstail,[5] and a ball,
A top can I set, and drive it in his kind.
But would to God these hateful books all,
Were in a fire burnt to powder small,
Then might I lead my life always in play;
Which life God send me to my ending day.

MANHOOD

Manhood I am, therefore I me delight
To hunt and hawk, to nourish up and feed
The greyhound to the course, the hawk to the flight,
And to bestride a good and lusty steed.
These things become a very man indeed,
Yet thinketh this boy his peevish game sweeter
But what, no force, his reason is no better.

VENUS AND CUPID

Whoso ne'er knoweth the strength, power, and might
Of Venus and me, her little son Cupid
Thou manhood shalt a mirror be aright
By us subdued for all thy great pride,

4. **Editor's Note:** Here, and in the pages following, glosses have been added to clarify obscure or obsolete expressions. "Quoit," *a small, discus-like iron ring.*

5. "Cockstail," *a stick thrown at cocks.*

My fiery dart pierceth thy tender side.
Now thou which once despised children small
Shall wax a child again and be my thrall.

AGE

Old age am I with locks thin and hoar,
Of our short life the last and best part
Wise and discreet, the public weal therefore
I help to rule, to my labor and smart.
Therefore Cupid withdraw thy fiery dart
Chargeable matters shall of love oppress
Thy childish game, and idle business.

DEATH

Though I be foul, ugly, lean, and misshape,
Yet there is none in all this world wide,
That may my power withstand or escape,
Therefore sage father greatly magnified,
Descend from your chair, set apart your pride,
Vouchsafe to lend (though it be to your pain)
To me a fool, some of your wise brain.

FAME

Fame I am called, marvel you nothing,
Though I with tongues am compassed all round,
For in voice of people is my chief living.
Oh cruel death, thy power I confound.
When thou a noble man has brought to ground
Maugre[6] thy teeth, to live cause him shall I,
Of people in perpetual memory.

6. "Maugre," meaning *in spite of.*

TIME

I, whom thou seest with horyloge[7] in hand,
Am named Time, the lord of every hour,
I shall in space destroy both sea and land.
Oh simple Fame, how darest thou man honor,
Promising of his name an endless flower?
Who may in the world have a name eternal,
When I shall in process destroy the world and all?

ETERNITY

Me needeth not to boast, I am Eternity,
The very name signifieth well,
That mine empire infinite shall be.
Thou mortal Time every man can tell,
Art nothing else but the mobility
Of sun and moon changing in every degree,
When they shall leave their course thou shalt be brought
For all thy pride and boasting unto naught.

THE POET[8]

Has fictas quemcunque iuvat spectare figuras,

---

7. "Horyloge," meaning *hourglass*.
8. **Editor's Note:** This last stanza was not included in the first edition of *Lyra Martyrum*. These Latin verses read:

> "Whoever delights himself in gazing at these figures, and even thinks that they accurately depict man with marvelous skill, can also delight his soul with true things in the same way that he gratifies his eyes on the images. For he will see how the uncertain goods of the ephemeral world do not come so quickly as they swiftly fade away. Joys, praise, honor and all things are overturned; what remains forever except God's love? Therefore, men, henceforth place no trust in trivial matters, and no expectations in a fleeting good. Present your prayers to the eternal God, who will bestow upon us the gift of everlasting life."

Translated by Joshua Avery, in "The Pageant of Life (1492–1501)," ed. Travis Curtwright (Irving, TX: Center for Thomas More Studies, 2007), pp. 4–5, available at https://www.thomasmorestudies.org/docs/Pageant_Life.pdf (accessed December 1, 2019).

Sed mira veros quas putat arte homines,
Ille potest veris, animum sic pascere rebus,
Ut pictis oculos pascit imaginibus.
Namque videbit uti fragilis bona lubrica mundi,
Tam cito non veniunt, quam cito pretereunt.
Gaudia laus & honor, celeri pede omnia cedunt,
Qui manet excepto semper amore dei?
Ergo homines, leuibus iamiam diffidite rebus,
Nulla recessuro spes adhibenda bono.
Qui dabit eternam nobis pro munere vitam,
In permansuro ponite vota deo.

Lamentation on the Death of Queen Elizabeth

Wife of King Henry VII and Mother of Henry VIII

Oh ye that put your trust and confidence,
In worldly joy and frail prosperity,
That so live here as ye should never hence,
Remember death and look here upon me.
Example I think there can no better be.
Your self knows well that in this realm was I,
Your queen but late, and, lo, now here I lie.

Was I not born of old worthy lineage?
Was not my mother queen, my father king?
Was I not a king's wife in marriage?
Had I not plenty of every pleasant thing?
Merciful God this is a strange reckoning:
Riches, honor, wealth, and ancestry,
Hath me forsaken and, lo, now here I lie.

If worship might have kept me, I had not gone.
If wit might me have saved, I needed not to fear.
If money might have helped, I lacked none.
But, Oh good God, what availeth all this gear?
When death is come, thy mighty messenger,
Obey we must, there is no remedy
Me hath he summoned, and, lo, now here I lie.

Yet was I late promised otherwise,
This year to live in wealth and delectation.
Lo where to commeth thy blandishing promise,
Oh false astrology and divination,
Of God's secrets making thyself so wise?

How true is for this year thy prophecy?
The year yet lasteth, and, lo, now here I lie.

Oh brittle wealth, all full of bitterness,
Thy single pleasure doubled is with pain.
Account my sorrow first and my distress,
In sundry ways, and reckon there again
The joy that I have had, and I dare maintain,
For all my honor, endured yet have I,
More woe then wealth, and, lo, now here I lie.

Where are our castles, where now are our towers?
Goodly Richmond, son art thou gone from me,
At Westminster that costly work of yours,
Mine own dear lord now shall I never see.
Almighty God, vouchsafe to grant that ye,
For you and your children well, may edify.
My palace builded is, and, lo, now here I lie.

Adieu my own dear spouse, my worthy lord,
The faithful love, that did us both combine,
In marriage and peaceful concord,
Into your hands here I clean resign,
To be bestowed upon your children and mine,
First were you father, and now must ye supply
The mother's part also, for, lo, now here I lie.

Farewell my daughter lady Margaret.
God wot full oft it grieved hath my mind,
That ye should go where we should seldom meet.
Now am I gone, and have left you behind.
Oh mortal folk that we be very blind,
What we least fear, full oft it is most nigh,
From you depart I first, and, lo, now here I lie.

Farewell Madame, my lord's worthy mother,
Comfort your son, and be ye of good cheer,
Take all a worth, for it will be no other.
Farewell my daughter Katherine, late the fere,[9]
To prince Arthur mine own child so dear,
It booteth not for me to weep or cry,
Pray for my soul, for, lo, now here I lie.

Adieu Lord Henry, my loving son, adieu.
Our Lord increase your honor and estate,
Adieu my daughter Mary bright of hue.
God make you virtuous, wise, and fortunate.
Adieu sweet heart, my little daughter Kate,
Thou shalt, sweet babe, such is thy destiny,
Thy mother never know, for, lo, now here I lie.

Lady Cecily, Anne, and Katherine,
Farewell my well-beloved sisters three,
Oh Lady Briget other sister mine,
Lo, here, the end of worldly vanity.
Now well are ye that earthly folly flee,
And heavenly things love and magnify,
Farewell and pray for me, for, lo, now here I lie.

Adieu my lord, adieu my ladies all,
Adieu my faithful servants every one.
Adieu my commons whom I never shall
See in this world. Wherefore to thee alone,
Immortal God verily three and one,
I me commend. Thy infinite mercy,
Show to thy servant now, for, lo, now here I lie.

9. "Fere," meaning *spouse*.

The Book of Fortune

THE WORDS OF FORTUNE TO THE PEOPLE

Mine high estate, power, and authority,
If ye not know, ensearch and ye shall spy,
That riches, worship, wealth, and dignity,
Joy, rest, and peace, and all thing finally,
That any pleasure or profit may come by,
To man's comfort, aid, and sustenance,
Is all at my device and ordinance.

Without my favor there is nothing won.
Many a matter have I brought at last
To good conclusion, that madly was begun,
And many a purpose, bounden sure and fast
With wise provision, I have overcast.
Without good chance there may no wit suffice,
Better is to be fortunate than wise.

And therefore hath there some men been 'fore this,
My deadly foes, and written many a book
To my dispraise. And other cause there's not,
But for me list not friendly on them look,
Thus like the fox they fare, that once forsook
The pleasant grapes, and 'gan for to defy them,
Because he lept and yet could not come nigh them.

But let them write—their labor is in vain,
For well ye wot, mirth, honor, and riches,
Much better is than penury and pain.
The needy wretch that lingereth in distress,
Without mine help is ever comfortless,

A weary burden odious and loath,
To all the world, and e'en to himself both.

But he that by my favor may ascend
To mighty power and excellent degree,
A common weal to govern and defend,
O in how blessed condition standeth he:
Himself in honor and felicity,
And over that, may further and increase,
A region whole in joyful rest and peace.

Now in this point there is no more to say,
Each man hath of himself the governance.
Let every wight then follow his own way.
And he that out of poverty and mischance,
List for to live, and will himself enhance,
In wealth and riches, come forth and wait on me;
And he that will be a beggar, let him be.

TO THEM THAT TRUST IN FORTUNE

Thou that art proud of honor, shape, or kin,
That heapest up this wretched world's treasure,
Thy fingers shrined with gold, thy tawny skin,
With fresh apparel garnished out of measure,
And wishest to have fortune at thy pleasure,
Cast up thine eye, and look how baffling chance,
Deceives her men with change and variance.

Sometimes she looks as lovely, fair, and bright,
As goodly Venus, mother of Cupid.
She becketh and she smileth on every wight.
But this cheer feigned, may not long abide.

There commeth a cloud, and farewell all our pride.
Like any serpent she beginneth to swell,
And looketh as fierce as any fury of hell.

Yet for all that we changeful men are fain
(So wretched is our nature and so blind)
As soon as Fortune list to laugh again,
With fair countenance and deceitful mind,
To crouch and kneel and gape after the wind.
Not one or twain, but thousands in a rout,
Like swarming bees come flickering her about.

Then as a bait she bringeth forth her ware,
Silver, gold, rich pearl, and precious stone,
On which the massed people gaze and stare,
And gape therefore, as dogs do for the bone.
Fortune at them laugheth, and in her throne
Amid her treasure and wavering riches,
Proudly she rules as lady and empress.

Fast by her side doth weary Labor stand,
Pale Fear also, and Sorrow all bewept,
Disdain and Hatred on that other hand,
Eke restless watch from sleep with travail kept,
His eyes drowsy and looking as he slept.
Before her standeth Danger and Envy,
Flattery, Deceit, Mischief and Tyranny.

About her commeth all the world to beg.
He asketh land, and he to pass would bring
This toy and that, and all not worth an egg;
He would in love prosper above all thing;
He kneeleth down and would be made a king;

He recketh not so he may money have,
Though all the world account him for a knave.

Lo thus ye see diverse heads, diverse wits.
Fortune, alone as diverse as they all,
Unstable here and there among them flits:
And at aventure down her gifts fall,
Catch who so may she throweth great and small
Not to all men, as commeth sun or dew,
But for the most part, all among a few.

And yet her changeful gifts long may not last.
He that she gave them, looketh proud and high.
She whirleth about and plucketh away as fast,
And giveth them to another by and bye.
And thus from man to man continually,
She useth to give and take, and slyly toss
One man to winning of another's loss.

And when she robbeth one, down goeth his pride;
He wepeth and waileth and curseth her full sore.
But he that receveth it, on that other side,
Is glad, and blesseth her often times therefore.
But in a while when she loveth him no more,
She glideth from him, and her gifts too,
And he her curseth as other fools are wont to do.

Alas! the foolish people cannot cease,
To escape her wiles, till they the harm do feel.
About her always basely they press.
But lord! how he doth think himself full well,
That may set once his hands upon her wheel.
He holdeth fast, but upward as he flieth,
She whippeth her wheel about, and there he lieth.

Thus fell Julius, from his mighty power.
Thus fell Darius the worthy king of Perse.[10]
Thus fell Alexander the sovereign conqueror.
Thus many more than I may well rehearse.
Thus double Fortune, when she list reverse
Her changeful favor from them that in her trust,
She fleeth her way and layeth them in the dust.

She suddenly enhanceth them aloft.
And suddenly mischieveth all the flock.
The head that late lay easily and soft,
Instead of pillows lieth after on the block.
And yet alas the most cruel proud mock:
The dainty mouth that ladies kissed have,
She bringeth in case to kiss a knave.

Thus when she changeth her uncertain course,
Up starteth a knave, and down there falls a knight,
The beggar rich, and the rich man poor is.
Hatred is turned to love, love to despight.
This is her sport, thus proveth she her might.
Great boast she maketh if one be by her power,
Wealthy and wretched both within an hour.

Poverty, that of her gifts will no thing take,[11]
With merry cheer, she looketh on the masses,
And seeth how Fortune's household goeth to wrack.
Fast by her standeth the wise Socrates,
Aristippus, Pythagoras, and many a three

10. "Perse," meaning *Persia.*

11. **Editor's Note:** The following four stanzas were omitted from the original *Lyra Martyrum.* The source text that has been modernized here is in *The Yale Edition of the Complete Works f St. Thomas More,* vol. 1: *English Poems, The Life of Pico, The Last Things* (New Haven, CT: Yale University Press, 1997), pp. 38–39.

Of old philosophers. So too against the sun
Baketh him poor Diogenes in his tun.[12]

With her is Bias, whose country lacked defense,
And once of their foes they stood in doubt,
That each man hastily 'gan to carry thence,
And asked him why he naught carried out.
"I bear," quoth he, "all mine with me about."
Wisdom he meant, not Fortune's brittle things;
For naught he counted his that he might lose.

Heraclitus too, list fellowship to keep
With glad Poverty; Democritus also;
Of which the first can never cease but weep,
To see how thick the blind people go,
With great labor to purchase care and woe.
That other laugheth to see the foolish apes,
How earnestly they walk about their japes.

Of this poor sect, it is the usage,
Only to take that which nature may sustain.
Banishing clean all other surplusage,
They be content, and of nothing complain.
No niggard too is of his good so fain,
But they ore pleasure have a thousand fold,
The secret drafts of nature to behold.

Set Fortune's servants by them and ye will,
That one is free, that other ever thrall;
That one content, that other never full;
That one in surety, that other like to fall.
Who lists to advise them both, perceive he shall,

12. "Tun," meaning *barrel*.

As great difference between them as we see
Between wretchedness and felicity.

Now have I showed you both: choose which ye list,
Stately Fortune, or humble Poverty:
That is to say, now lieth it in your fist,
To take here bondage, or free liberty.
But in this point, and ye do after me,
Draw you to fortune, and labor her to please,
If that ye think yourself too well at ease.

And first, upon thee lovely shall she smile,
And friendly on thee cast her wandering eyes,
Embrace thee in her arms, and for a while,
Put thee and keep thee in a fool's paradise:
And forthwith all what so thou list devise,
Thee will she grant it liberally—perhaps:
But for all that—beware of after-claps.

Reckon you never of her favor sure:
Ye may in clouds as easily track a hare,
Or in dry land cause fishes to endure,
And make the burning fire his heat to spare,
And all this world in compass to forfare
As her to make by craft or engine stable,
That of her nature is ever variable.

Serve her day and night as reverently
Upon thy knees as any servant may,
And in conclusion, what thou shalt win thereby
Shall not be worth thy service I dare say.
And yet look what she giveth thee to-day,
With labor won she shall haply tomorrow
Pluck it again out of thine hand with sorrow.

Wherefore if thou in safety wish to stand,
Take Poverty's part and let proud Fortune go,
Receive nothing that commeth from her hand:
Love morals and virtue: they be only those
Which double fortune may not take thee from.
Then mayst thou boldly defy her, turning Chance.
She can thee neither hinder nor advance.

But an thou wilt needs meddle with her treasure,
Trust not therein, and spend it liberally.
Bear thee not proud, nor take not out of measure.
Build not thine house on height up in the sky:
None falleth far, but he that climbeth high,
Remember nature sent thee hither bare,
The gifts of fortune count them borrowed ware.

TO THEM THAT SEEK FORTUNE

Whoso delighteth to proven and assay
Of wavering fortune the uncertain lot,
If that the answer please you not alway
Blame ye not me: for I command you not
Fortune to trust, and eke full well ye wot,
I have of her no bridle in my fist,
She runneth loose, and turneth where she list.

The rolling dice in whom your luck doth stand,
With whose unhappy chance ye be so wroth,
Ye know yourself came never in mine hand.
Lo in this pond be fish and frogs both.
Cast in your net: but be you liefe[13] or loath,

13. "Liefe," meaning *glad*.

Hold you content as fortune doth assign:
For it is your own fishing and not mine.

And though in one chance fortune you offend,
Grudge not thereat, but bear a merry face.
In many another she shall it amend.
There is no man so far out of her grace,
But he sometime hath comfort and solace:
Nor none gain so far forth in her favor,
That is full satisfied with her behavior.

Fortune is stately, solemn, proud, and high:
And riches giveth, to have service therefore.
The needy beggar catcheth an halfpenny:
Some man a thousand pounds, some less, some more.
But for all that she keepeth ever in store,
From every man some parcel of his will,
That he may pray therefore and serve her still.

Some man hath goods, but children hath he none,
Some man hath both, but he can get no health.
Some hath all three, but up to Honor's throne
Can he not creep, by no manner of stealth.
To some she sendeth children, riches, wealth,
Honour, worship, and reverence all his life:
But yet she pincheth him with a shrewish wife.

Then for as much as it is fortune's guise,
To grant no man all things that he will ask,
But as herself list order and devise,
Doth every man his part divide and tax,
I counsel you each one truss up your packs
And take nothing at all, or be content,
With such reward as Fortune hath you sent.

All things in this book that ye shall read,[14]
Do as ye list, there shall no man you bind
Them to believe, as surely as your creed.
But, notwithstanding, certes is my mind
I durst well swear, as true shall ye them find,
In every point each answer by and by,
As are the judgements of astronomy.

14. **Editor's Note:** This stanza was omitted from the original *Lyra Martyrum*. The source text that has been modernized here is in *The Yale Edition of the Complete Works of St. Thomas More*, vol. 1: *English Poems, The Life of Pico, The Last Things*, pp. 42–43.

Twelve Rules of John Picus, Earl of Mirandula

PARTLY EXCITING, PARTLY DIRECTING A MAN IN SPIRITUAL BATTLE

If we refuse the Way of Virtue for that it is Painful,
for the Like Cause ought we to refuse the Way of Sin

Whoso to virtue esteemeth hard the way
Because we must have war continual
Against the world, the flesh, the devil, that aye
Enforce themself to make us bond and thrall,
Let him remember that choose what may he shall
Even after the world, yet must he need sustain
Sorrow, adversity, labor, grief, and pain.

THE SECOND RULE

Think in this wretched world's busy woe
The battle more sharp and longer is I wis[15]
With more labor and less fruit also
In which the end of labor labor is:
And when the world hath left us after this
Void of all virtue: the reward when we die
Is nought but fire and pain perpetually.

THE THIRD RULE

Consider well that folly it is and vain

15. "Wis," meaning *know*.

To look for heaven with pleasure and delight.
Since Christ our Lord and sovereign captain
Ascended never but by manly fight
And bitter passion; then were it no right
That any servant, ye will yourself record,
Should stand in better condition than his lord.

THE FOURTH RULE

Think how that we not only should not grudge
But eke be glad and joyful of this fight,
And long therefore although we could not judge
How that thereby redound unto us might
Any profit, but only for delight
To be conformed and like in some behavior
To Jesu Christ our blessed Lord and Savior.

As often as thou dost war and strive,
By the resistance of any sinful motion,
Against any of thy sensual wits five,
Cast in thy mind as oft with good devotion
How thou resemblest Christ: as with sour potion
If thou pain thy taste: remember therewithal
How Christ for thee tasted eysell[16] and gall.

If thou withdraw thine hands and forbear
The ravin[17] of anything: remember then
How his innocent hands nailed were.

16. "Eysell," meaning *vinegar*.
17. "Ravin," meaning *theft*.

If thou be tempt with pride: think how that when
He was in form of God, yet of a bondman
He took the shape and humbled himself for thee
To the most odious and vile death of a tree.

Consider when thou are moved to be wroth
He who that was God, and of all men the best,
Seeing himself scorned and scourged both,
And as a thief between two thieves threst
With all rebuke and shame: yet from his breast
Came never sign of wrath or of disdain
But patiently endured all the pain.

Thus every snare and engine of the devil
If thou this wise peruse them by and by:
There can be none so cursed or so evil
But to some virtue thou mayst it apply.
For oft thou shalt, resisting valiantly
The fiend's might and subtle fiery dart,
Our Savior Christ resemble in some part.

THE FIFTH RULE

Remember well that we in no wise must
Neither in the foresaid espiritual armor.
Nor any other remedy put our trust,
But only in the virtue of our Savior:
For he it is by whose mighty power
The world was vanquished and his prince cast out
Which reigned before in all the earth about.

In him let us trust to overcome all evil,
In him let us put our hope and confidence

To subdue the flesh and master the devil,
To him be all honor and lowly reverence;
Oft should we require with all our diligence
With prayer, with tears, and lamentable plaints:
The aid of his grace and of his holy saints.

THE SIXTH RULE

One sin vanquished, look thou not tarry,
But lie in await for another very hour,
For as a fierce lion, the fiend, our adversary,
Runneth about seeking whom he may devour;
Wherefore continually upon thy tower,
Lest thee he unpurveyed and unready catch,
Thou must with the prophet stand and keep watch.

THE SEVENTH RULE

Enforce thyself not only for to stand
Unvanquished against the devil's might
But over that take valiantly on hand
To vanquish him and put him unto flight:
And that is when of the same deed, thought or sight
By which he would have thee with sin contract,
Thou takest occasion of some good virtuous act.

Sometime he secretly casteth in thy mind
Some laudable deed to stir thee to pride,
As vain glory maketh many a man blind.
But let humility be thy sure guide,
Thy good work to God let it be applied,

Think it not thine but a gift of his
Of whose grace undoubtedly all goodness is.

THE EIGHTH RULE

In time of battle so put thyself in preace[18]
As though thou shouldest after that victory
Enjoy forever a perpetual peace:
For God of his goodness and liberal mercy
May grant the gift, and eke thy proud enemy,
Confounded and rebuked by thy battle,
Shall thee no more haply for very shame assail.

But when thou mayest once the triumph obtain,
Prepare thyself and trim thee in thy gear
As thou shouldest incontinent fight again,
For if thou be ready the devil will thee fear:
Wherefore in any wise so even thou thee bear
That thou remember and have ever in memory
In victory battle, in battle victory.

THE NINTH RULE

If thou think thyself well fenced and sure
Against every subtle suggestion of vice,
Consider frail glass may no distress endure,
And great adventurers oft curse the dice:
Jeopard not too far therefore an ye be wise,
But evermore eschew the occasions of sin,
For he that loveth peril shall perish therein.

18. "Preace," meaning *trim, fighting condition.*

THE TENTH RULE

In all temptation withstand the beginning:
The cursed infants of wretched Babylon
To suffer them wax is a jeopardous thing:
Beat out their brains therefore at the stone:
Perilous is the canker that catcheth the bone:
Too late cometh the medicine if thou let the sore
By long continuance increase more and more.

THE ELEVENTH RULE

Though in the time of the battle and war
The conflict seem bitter, sharp and sour,
Yet consider it is more pleasure far
Over the devil to be a conqueror
Than is in the use of thy beastly pleasure:
Of virtue more joy the conscience hath within
Than outward the body of all his filthy sin.

In this point many men err for negligence
For they compare not the joy of the victory
To the sensual pleasure of their concupiscence,
But like rude beasts unadvisedly
Lacking discretion they compare and apply
Of their foul sin the voluptuous delight
To the laborious travail of the conflict and fight.

And yet alas he that oft hath known
What grief it is by long experience
Of his cruel enemy to be overthrown,
Should once at the leastwise do his diligence
To prove and essay with manly defense

What pleasure there is, what honor, peace, and rest
In glorious victory, triumph, and conquest.

THE TWELFTH RULE

Though thou be tempted, despair thee nothing:
Remember the glorious apostle Saint Paul
When he had seen God in his perfect being,
Lest such revelation should his heart extol,
His flesh was suffered rebel against his soul:
This did almighty God of his goodness provide
To preserve his servant from the danger of pride.

And here take heed that he whom God did love,
And for his most especial vessel chose,
Ravished into the third heaven above,
Yet stood in peril lest pride might him depose:
Well ought we then our hearts fence and close
Against vain glory, the mother of reprief[19]
The very crop and root of all mischief.

Against this pomp and wretched world's gloss
Consider how Christ the Lord, sovereign power,
Humbled himself for us unto the cross:
And peradventure death within one hour
Shall us bereave wealth, riches and honor:
And bring us down full low both small and great
To vile carrion and wretched worm's meat.

19. "Reprieve," meaning *reproof.*

The Twelve Weapons of Spiritual Battle

The pleasure little and short.
The follower's grief and heaviness.
The loss of a better thing.
This life a dream and a shadow.
The death at our hand and unaware.
The fear of impenitent departing.
Eternal reward, eternal pain.
The nature and dignity of man.
The peace of a good mind.
The great benefits of God.
The painful cross of Christ.
The witness of martyrs and
example of saints.

THE PLEASURE LITTLE AND SHORT

Consider well the pleasure that thou hast,
Stand it in touching or in wanton sight,
In vain smell or in thy lecherous taste,
Or finally, in whatsoever delight
Occupied is thy wretched appetite:
Thou shalt it find, when thou hast all cast
Little, simple, short, and suddenly past.

THE FOLLOWER'S GRIEF AND HEAVINESS

Any good work if thou with labor do,
The labor goeth, the goodness doth remain:
If thou do evil with pleasure joined thereto,
The pleasure which thine evil work doth contain
Glideth his way, thou must him not restrain:
The evil then in thy breast cleaveth behind
With grudge of heart and heaviness of mind.

THE LOSS OF A BETTER THING

When thou laborest thy pleasure for to buy
Upon the price look thou well thee advise,
Thou sellest thy soul therefore even by and by
To thy most utter despiteous enemies:
O mad merchant, O foolish merchandise,
To buy a trifle, O childish reckoning,
And pay therefore so dear a precious thing!

THIS LIFE A DREAM AND A SHADOW

This wretched life, the trust and confidence
Of whose continuance maketh us bold to sin,
Thou perceivest well by experience,
Since that hour in which it did begin,
It holdeth on the course and will not lin,[20]
But fast it runneth on and passen shall
As doth a dream or shadow on the wall.

DEATH AT OUR HAND AND UNAWARE

Consider well that both by night and day,
While that we busily provide and care
For our disport, our revel, and our play,
For pleasant melody and dainty fare,
Death stealeth on full slyly, unaware
He lieth at hand and shall us all surprise,
We wot not when or where, nor in what wise.

20. "Lin," meaning *cease.*

FEAR OF IMPENITENT DEPARTING

If thou shouldst God offend, think how therefore
Thou were forthwith in very jeopardous case:
For haply thou shouldst not live an hour more
Thy sin to cleanse, and though thou haddest space,
Yet peradventure shouldst thou lack the grace:
Well ought we then be feared to do offence
Impenitent lest we departen hence.

ETERNAL REWARD, ETERNAL PAIN

Thou seest this world is but a thoroughfare,
See thou behave thee wisely with thine host;
Hence must thou needs depart naked and bare,
And after thy desert look to what cost
Thou art conveyed at such time as thy ghost
From this wretched carcass shall dissever:
Be it joy or pain, endure it shall forever.

THE NATURE AND DIGNITY OF MAN

Remember how God hath made thee reasonable
Like unto his image and figure,
And for thee suffered pains intolerable
That he for angel never would endure.
Regard, Oh man, thine excellent nature;
Thou that with angel art made to be equal,
For very shame be not the devil's thrall.

THE PEACE OF A GOOD MIND

Why lovest thou so this brittle world's joy?
Take all the mirth, take all the fantasies,
Take every game, take every wanton toy,
Take every sport that men can thee devise:
And among them all on warranties
Thou shaft no pleasure comparable find
To th' inward gladness of a virtuous mind.

THE GREAT BENEFITS OF GOD

Beside that God thee bought and formed both
Many a benefit hast thou received of his:
Though thou have moved him often to be wroth
Yet he thee kept hath and brought thee up to this,
And daily calleth upon thee to his bliss:
How mayst thou then to him unloving be
That ever hath been so loving unto thee?

THE PAINFUL CROSS OF CHRIST

When fierce temptations threat thy soul with loss,
Think on his passion and the bitter pain,
Think on the mortal anguish of the cross,
Think on Christ's blood let out at every vein,
Think of his precious heart all rent in twain;
For thy redemption think all this was wrought,
Nor be that lost which he so dearly bought.

---

21. "Eftsoon," meaning *quickly,* or *soon.*

THE WITNESS OF MARTYRS AND EXAMPLE OF SAINTS

Sin to withstand say not thou lackest might:
Such excuses tis but folly so to use;
The witness of saints, and martyrs' constant fight
Shall thee of slothful cowardice accuse:
God will thee help if thou do not refuse:
If other have stand or this thou mayst eftsoon[21]:
Nothing impossible is which ever hath been done.

The Twelve Properties or Conditions of a Lover

THE FIRST PROPERTY
TO LOVE ONE ALONE AND CONTEMN ALL OTHER FOR THAT ONE

The first point is to love but one alone,
And for that one all other to forsake:
For whoso loveth many loveth none:
The flood that is in many channels take
In each of them shall feeble streams make:
The love that is divided among many
Uneath[22] sufficeth that any part have any.

So thou that hast thy love set unto God
In thy remembrance this imprint and grave:
As he in sovereign dignity is odd,[23]
So will He in love no parting fellows have:
Love him therefore with all that He thee gave:
For body, soul, wit, cunning, mind, and thought,
Part will He none, but either all or naught.

THE SECOND PROPERTY
TO THINK HIM UNHAPPY THAT IS NOT WITH HIS LOVE

Of his love, lo, the sight and company
To the lover so glad and pleasant is,
That whoso hath the grace to come thereby
He judgeth him in perfect joy and bliss:

22. "Uneath," meaning *hardly.*
23. "Odd," meaning *unique.*

And whoso of that company doth miss,
Live he in never so prosperous estate,
He thinketh him wretched and unfortunate.

So should the lover of God esteem that he
While all the pleasure hath, mirth and disport,
Which in the world is possible to be,
Yet till the time that he may once resort
Unto that blessed, joyful, heavenly port
Where he of God may have the glorious sight,
Is void of perfect joy and sure delight

THE THIRD PROPERTY
TO ADORN HIMSELF FOR THE PLEASURE OF HIS LOVE

The third point of a perfect lover is
To make him fresh to see that all thing been
Appointed well and nothing set amiss
But all well fashioned, proper, goodly, clean:
That in his person there be nothing seen
In speech, apparel, gesture, look, or pace
That may offend or 'minish any grace.

So thou that wilt with God get into favor
Garnish thyself up in as goodly wise
As comely be, as honest in behavior
As it is possible for thee to devise:
I mean not hereby that thou shouldest arise
And in the glass upon thy body prowl,[24]
But with fair virtue to adorn thy soul.

24. "Prowl," meaning *search, look eagerly.*

THE FOURTH PROPERTY
TO SUFFER ALL THING, THOUGH IT BE DEATH, TO BE WITH HIS LOVE

If love be strong, hot, mighty, and fervent,
There may no trouble, grief, or sorrow fall,
But that the lover would be well content
All to endure and think it eke too small,
Though it were death, so he might wherewithal
The joyful presence of that person get
On whom he hath his heart and love yset.[25]

Thus should of God the lover be content
Any distress or sorrow to endure,
Rather than to be from God absent,
And glad to die, so that he may be sure
By his departing hence for to procure
After this valley dark, the heavenly light,
And of his love the glorious blessed sight.

THE FIFTH PROPERTY
TO DESIRE ALSO TO SUFFER HARM FOR HIS LOVE AND TO THINK THAT HURT SWEET

Not only a lover content is in his heart
But coveteth eke and longeth, to sustain
Some labor, incommodity, or smart,
Loss, adversity, trouble, grief, or pain:
And of his sorrow joyful is and fain,
And happy thinketh himself that he may take
Some misadventure for his lover's sake.

25. "Yset," meaning *set*.

Thus shouldest thou, that lovest God also,
In thine heart wish, covet, and be glad
To suffer for him trouble, pain, and woe:
For whom if thou be never so woe bestead,
Yet thou me shalt sustain (be not adread)
Half the dolor, grief, and adversity
That he already suffered hath for thee.

THE SIXTH PROPERTY
TO BE WITH HIS LOVE EVER AS HE MAY, IF NOT IN DEED, YET IN THOUGHT

The perfect lover longeth for to be
In presence of his love both night and day,
And if it haply so befall that he
May not as he would, he will yet as he may
Ever be with his love, that is to say,
Where his heavy body nil[26] be brought
He will be conversant in mind and thought.

Lo, in like manner the lover of God should,
At the least in such wise as he may,
If he may not in such wise as he would,
Be present with God and conversant alway;
For certes, whoso list, he may purvey,
Though all the world would him therefrom bereaven[27]
To bear his body in earth, his mind in heaven.

26. "Nil," meaning *will not.*

27. "Bereaven," meaning *separate.*

THE SEVENTH PROPERTY
TO LOVE ALL THINGS WHICH PERTAINETH UNTO HIS LOVE

There is no page or servant, most or least,
That doth upon his love attend and wait,
There is no little worm, no simple beast,
No none so small a trifle or conceit,
Lace, girdle, point,[28]or proper glove strait,
But that if to his love it have been near,
The lover trunks it precious, sweet and dear.

So every relic, image, or picture
That doth pertain to God's magnificence,
The lover of God should with all busy cure
Have it in love, honor, and reverence
And specially give them pre-eminence
Which daily done his blessed body wurche[29]
The quick relics, the ministers of his Church.

THE EIGHTH PROPERTY
TO COVET THE PRAISE OF HIS LOVE
AND NOT TO SUFFER ANY DISPRAISE

A very lover above all earthly thing
Coveteth and longeth evermore to hear
The honor, laud, commendation, and praising,
And everything that may the fame clear
Of his love: he may in no manner
Endure to hear that therefrom mighten vary
Or anything sound into the contrary.

---

28. "Point," meaning *fastening.*
29. "Wurche," meaning *cause to work, become active.*

The lover of God should covet in like wise
To hear his honor, worship, laud, and praise,
Whose sovereign goodness no heart may comprise,
Whom hell, earth, and all the heaven obeys,
Whose perfect lover ought by no manner ways
To suffer the cursed words of blasphemy,
Or anything spoken of God unreverently.

THE NINTH PROPERTY
TO BELIEVE OF HIS LOVE ALL THINGS EXCELLENT AND TO DESIRE THAT ALL FOLK SHOULD THINK THE SAME

A very lover believeth in his mind
On whomsoever he hath his heart ybent,
That in that person men may nothing find
But honorable, worthy, and excellent,
And eke surmounting far in his intent
All other that he hath known by sight or name:
And would that every man should think the same.

Of God, likewise, so wonderful and high,
All thing esteem and judge his lover ought,
So reverence, worship, honor, and magnify,
That all the creatures in this world ywrought,
In comparison should he set at nought,
And glad be if he might the mean devise
That all the world would thinken in like wise.

THE TENTH PROPERTY
TO WEEP OFTEN FOR HIS LOVE: IN PRESENCE FOR JOYS, IN ABSENCE FOR SORROW

The lover is of color dead and pale;
There will no sleep into his eyes stalk;
He favoreth neither meat, wine, nor ale;
He mindeth not what men about him talk;
But eat he, drink he, sit, lie down, or walk,
He burneth ever as it were with a fire
In the fervent heat of his desire.

Here should the lover of God ensample take
To have him continually in remembrance,
With him in prayer and meditation wake,
While other play, revel, sing, and dance:
None earthly joy, disport, or vain pleasance
Should him delight, or anything remove
His ardent mind from God, his heavenly love.

THE ELEVENTH PROPERTY
TO LANQUISH EVER, AND EVER TO BURN
IN THE DESIRE OF HIS LOVE

Diversely passioned is the lover's heart:
Now pleasant hope, now dread and grievous fear,
Now perfect bliss, now bitter sorrow smart;
And whether his love be with him or elsewhere,
Oft from his eyes there falleth many a tear,
For very joy, when they together be;
When they be sundered, for adversity.

Like affections moveth eke the breast
Of God's lover in prayer and meditation:
When that his love liketh in him rest
With inward gladness of pleasant contemplation,
Out break the tears for joy and delectation;

And when his love list eft to part him fro,[30]
Out break the tears again for pain and woe.

THE TWELFTH PROPERTY
TO SERVE HIS LOVE, NOTHING THINKING OF ANY REWARD OR PROFIT

A very lover will his love obey:
His joy it is and all his appetite
To pain himself in all that ever he may,
That person in whom he set hath his delight
Diligently to serve both day and night
For very love, without any regard
To any profit, guerdon, or reward.

So thou likewise that hast thine heart yset
Upward to God, so well thyself endeavor,
So studiously that nothing may thee let
Not for his service any wise dissever:
Freely look eke thou serve that thereto never
Trust of reward or profit do thee bind,
But only faithful heart and loving mind.

Wageless to serve, three things us should move:
First, if the service self be desirable:
Second, if they whom that we serve and love
Be very good and very amiable:
Thirdly, of reason be we serviceable
Without the gaping after any more
To such as have done much for us before.

30. "List eft to part him fro," meaning *desires afterward to part from him.*

Serve God for love, then, not for hope of meed[31]:
What service may so desirable be
As where all turneth to thy own speed?
Who is so good, so lovely eke as he
Who hath already done so much for thee,
As he that first thee made, and on the rood[32]
Eft thee redeemed with his own precious blood?

31. "Meed," meaning *payment* or *reward*.

32. "Rood," meaning [*Christ's*] *cross*.

A Prayer of Picus Mirandula unto God
(Done into English by Sir Thomas More)

O holy God of dreadful majesty,
Verily one in three and three in one,
Whom angels serve, whose work all creatures be,
Which heaven and earth directest all alone:
We thee beseech, good Lord, with woeful moan,
Spare us wretches and wash away our guilt
That we be not by thy just anger spilt.

In strait balance of rigorous judgment
If thou shouldst our sin ponder and weigh,
Who able were to bear thy punishment?
The whole engine of all this world, I say,
The engine that enduren shall for aye,
With such examination might not stand
Space of a moment in thine angry hand.

Who is not born in sin original?
Who doth not actual sin in sundry wise?
But thou, good Lord, art he that sparest all,
With piteous mercy tempering justice;
For as thou dost rewards us devise
Above our merit, so dost thou dispense
Thy punishment far under our offense.

More is thy mercy far than all our sin:
To give them also that unworthy be
More godly is, and more mercy therein.
Howbeit, worthy enough are they, pardee,[33]
Be they never so unworthy, whom that he

33. "Pardee," meaning *indeed.*

List to accept: which wheresoever he taketh
Whom he unworthy findeth worthy maketh.

Wherefore, good Lord, that aye merciful art,
Unto thy grace and sovereign dignity
We silly[34] wretches cry with humble heart:
Our sins forget and our malignity,
With piteous eyes of thy benignity
Friendly look on us once, thine own, we be,
Servants or sinners whether it liketh thee.

Sinners, if thou our crime behold, certain,
Our crime the work of our uncourteous mind,
But if thy gifts thou behold again,
Thy gifts noble, wonderful and kind,
Thou shalt us then the same persons find
Which are to thee, and have been long space
Servants by nature, children by thy grace.

But this thy goodness wringeth us, alas,
For we whom grace had made thy children dear,
Are made thy guilty folk by our trespass;
Sin hath us guilty made this many a year.
But let thy grace, thy grace that hath no peer,
Of our offence surmounten all the preace,[35]
That in our sin thine honor may increase.

For though thy wisdom, though thy sovereign power,
May otherwise appear sufficiently
As things which thy creatures every hour
All with one voice declare and testify,

34. "Silly," meaning *simple.*

35. "Preace," meaning *burden, pressure.*

Thy goodness yet, thy singular mercy,
Thy piteous heart, thy gracious indulgence
Nothing so clearly showeth as our offence.

What but our sin hath showed that mighty love
Which able was thy dreadful majesty
To drawn down into earth from heaven above
And crucify God, that we, poor wretches we,
Should from our filthy sin uncleansed be
With blood and water of thine own side,
That streamèd from thy blessed wounds wide?

Thy love and pity, thus, Oh heavenly King,
Our evil maketh matter of thy goodness,
Oh love, Oh pity, our wealth aye providing,
Oh goodness serving thy servants in distress,
Oh love, Oh pity, well nigh now thankless,
Oh goodness, mighty, gracious and wise,
And yet almost vanquished with our vice.

Grant, I thee pray, such heat into mine heart
That to this love of thine may be equal;
Grant me from Satan's service to astart,[36]
With whom me rueth so long to have be thrall;
Grant me, good Lord and Creator of all,
The flame to quench of all sinful desire
And in thy love set all mine heart afire:

That when the journey of this deadly life
My silly ghost hath finishèd, and thence
Departen must without his fleshly wife,
Alone into his Lord's high presence

36. "Astart," meaning *escape*.

He may thee find, Oh well of indulgence,
In thy lordship not as a lord, but rather
As a very tender loving father.

Amen.

Poems to Fortune[37]

(Written in the Tower of London, c. 1535)

LEWIS THE LOST LOVER

Ay, flattering Fortune, look thou never so fair,
Nor never so pleasantly begin to smile,
As though thou wouldst my ruin all repair,
During my life thou shalt me not beguile.
Trust shall I God, to enter in awhile
His haven of heaven sure and uniform:
Ever after thy calm, look I for a storm.

DAVEY THE DICER

Long was I, Lady Luck, your serving man,
And now have I lost again all that I got,
Wherefore when I think on you now and then,
And in my mind remember this and that,
Ye may not blame me though I beshrew[38] your cat,
But in faith I bless you again a thousand times,
For lending me now some leisure to make rhymes.

37. **Editor's Note:** The subtitles for these two poems were not included in the original edition of *Lyra Martyrum*. They are drawn from *The Yale Edition of the Complete Works of St. Thomas More*, vol. 1: *English Poems, The Life of Pico, The Last Things* (New Haven, CT: Yale University Press, 1997), pp. 45-46.

38. "Beshrew," meaning *wish ill upon*.

A Godly Meditation

(Written in the margins of More's prayer book while he was prisoner in the Tower of London, 1534–1535)

Give me thy grace, good Lord,
To set the world at naught;

To set my mind fast upon thee
And not to hang upon the blast of men's mouths;

To be content to be solitary,
Not to long for worldly company;

Little and little utterly to cast off the world
And rid my mind of all the business thereof;

Not to long to hear of any worldly things,
But that the hearing of worldly fantasies may be to
me displeasant;

Gladly to be thinking of God,
Piteously to call for his help;

To lean unto the comfort of God,
Busily to labor to love him;

To know mine own vilitie[39] and wretchedness,
To humble and meeken[40] myself under the mighty hand of
God;

39. "Vility," meaning *vileness of character.*

40. "Meeken," meaning *to make meek.*

To bewail my sins passed,
For the purging of them, patiently to suffer adversity;

Gladly to bear my purgatory here,
To be joyful of tribulations;

To walk the narrow way that leadeth to life,
To bear the cross with Christ;

To have the last things in remembrance,
To have ever before mine eye, my death, which is ever
at hand;

To make death no stranger to me,
To foresee and consider the everlasting fire of hell;

To pray for pardon before the judge come,
To have continually in mind, the Passion which Christ
suffered for me;

For His benefits unceasingly to give him thanks,
To buy the time again that I before have lost;

To abstain from vain confabulations.
To eschew light foolish mirth and gladness;

Recreations not necessary, to cut off,
Of worldly substance, friends, liberty, life and all, to set the loss
at right naught for the winning of Christ;

To think my most enemies my best friends,
For the brethren of Joseph could never have done him so much
good with their love and favor, as they did with their malice
and hatred.

These minds are more to be desired of every man than all the
treasure of all the princes
And kings, Christian and heathen, were it gathered and laud
together all upon one heap.

VENERABLE PHILIP HOWARD, EARL OF ARUNDEL

(1557–OCTOBER 15, 1595)

PHILIP HOWARD WAS BORN into a family that was firmly situated in the very highest circles of English nobility, but was in nearly constant conflict with the Tudor monarchs. Philip's grandfather was Henry Howard, Earl of Surrey, famous today as one of the most significant early poets of the English Renaissance, and one of the very first to write sonnets in English. Despite the fact that he was first cousin to two of Henry VIII's wives, including Anne Boleyn, Henry Howard angered the king and was beheaded in 1547 for supposedly scheming to take the throne. His son, Thomas Howard, was raised a Protestant, but had some Catholic sympathies, and he plotted to assassinate Queen Elizabeth, and liberate, marry and enthrone Mary, Queen of Scots. When the plot came to light, Thomas Howard was beheaded for treason in 1572. Philip Howard was the third Howard heir in a row to be condemned to death; in his case, however, his only crime was having converted to Catholicism and refusing to attend the Church of England services.

Philip Howard's mother died a few months after she gave birth to him in 1557, likely from labor complications. His father married twice more, each time marrying well and gaining wealth and connections, but his second wife died in 1564 and his third wife died in 1567. By the time Philip was ten years old, he had lost his mother and two stepmothers. His second stepmother was a widow by the time she married Philip's father, and she brought four of her own children into the family. This proved deeply consequential for Philip, as his father betrothed him—at age twelve—to one of these children, Anne, in 1569. The marriage was solemnized when Philip and Anne both reached fourteen (then regarded as the age of consent). It appears that Thomas Howard urged the solemnization of the marriage while he was imprisoned in the Tower of London, fearing that otherwise Elizabeth might ignore the betrothal. The next year, Thomas was beheaded for treason.

Despite these tempestuous years, Philip advanced in his studies, and spent several years at Cambridge University, where he showed some promise as a young scholar. He then became a courtier in Elizabeth's court, and in his efforts to win her favor, spent lavish amounts of money. He eventually accrued great debts despite his fortune and enormous estates, but he did not succeed with Elizabeth, and he made several enemies in court while also angering some of his relatives. While Philip was fruitlessly pursuing the rewards of the courtly life, his wife was living in the country. Anne, already sympathetic towards Catholicism due to her childhood education (which was overseen by Catholics) converted to Catholicism herself. When Philip finally retired from the court in 1580, in debt and in disgrace, he found his quiet wife openly and firmly declaring her Catholic faith. Philip's disappointments in the court evidently helped prepare him for conversion, and he was further moved when he attended public disputations between the Jesuit Edmund Campion and several prominent divines of the Church of England in September of 1581. Campion, although he had been tortured in prison and given no books or time to prepare for the disputations, was judged by many who attended to have had the upper hand in the arguments. Philip Howard thought so too, finding Campion's case in defense of the Catholic Church so strong that he could no longer remain Protestant. He was formally brought into the Church by the Jesuit William Weston in 1584.

For a brief period following Philip's conversion, the Howards enjoyed a peaceful and close marriage, and Anne gave birth to their first child, Elizabeth. They devoted their considerable resources to assist persecuted Catholics and hunted priests, hiding them in their various houses and acting as liaisons between the priests who were secretly arriving from Douai and Rome and the Catholic families and communities throughout England. This activity did not go unnoticed, and Philip was questioned by the government and then placed under house arrest. Pressure against him mounted to such an extent that he thought it better to flee England and join the expatriate Catholics on the continent. Anne was pregnant with their second child, a boy, at this time, so Philip left without her, expecting her to be treated more leniently, and expecting to send for her when she could travel. His ship was searched just as it left the harbor, however, and he was sent to the Tower of London as a prisoner in April 1585.

Philip was charged with a variety of crimes, which included being a Catholic and harboring and conspiring with priests. He spent three years in prison without being brought to trial. Then, in 1588, following the destruction of the Spanish Armada, a fellow prisoner and priest reported, under torture, that Philip had asked him to pray for the success of the Armada. This was considered definitive proof of treason, and Philip was tried, convicted, and condemned to death in April 1589. Remarkably, the sentence was never enacted. Instead, Philip was simply left in prison, expecting that any day might bring his execution, and never told whether it would be carried out or if he might expect some clemency.

Confined for years in the Tower, Philip spent his time working on several spiritual and philosophical works, and in composing the poems that are included here. While he was imprisoned, Anne continued to use her greatly curtailed position and means to assist priests. She became a chief supporter of the Jesuit Robert Southwell, whose poetry is included in this anthology (pp. 123–62), and who wrote letters of comfort and counsel to Philip. Southwell would eventually be caught, condemned, and imprisoned in the Tower as well, although it is doubtful whether he and Philip were ever allowed to meet in person. Tradition holds, however, that Philip was allowed to keep a dog, who would run between the different prison cells, and would visit Southwell and carry his blessing back to Philip. Later depictions of Philip Howard often depict the dog, keeping him company in his cell.

Robert Southwell, although apprehended long after Philip, was executed while Philip lived on in uncertain limbo. In the walls of his own cell, Philip scratched the Latin phrase, *Quanto plus afflictiones pro Christo in hoc saeculo, tanto plus gloriae cum Christo in future* ("the more affliction we endure for Christ in this world, the more glory we will share with Christ in the next"). At last, in August 1595, after a full decade of imprisonment, Philip grew very sick, and wrote a letter to Queen Elizabeth asking for permission to see his wife and children one final time. She responded that if he attended Anglican services, she would release him and restore all of his property and titles to him. He refused. On October 15, 1595, he died from the sickness (or, as it was rumored, from poisoning). He never met his son, who was born after his arrest, although he was nearly ten years old when Philip died. Philip was widely regarded as a martyr, having suffered and lost all for his faith. Anne honored his memory throughout her long life, receiving permission from King James I in 1624 to move Philip's remains from the Tower chapel to Arundel Castle, where he was reinterred. Although Philip's fall had greatly impoverished her and the family, she continued to be an important supporter and patron of Catholic priests and writers until her death in 1630.

Sources and Further Reading:

Elzinga, J.G. "Howard, Philip [St. Philip Howard], thirteenth earl of Arundel (1557–1595)." In *Oxford Dictionary of National Biography*. Oxford: Oxford University Press, 2004.

Havens, Earle. "Notes from a Literary Underground: Recusant Catholics, Jesuit Priests, and Scribal Publication in Elizabethan England." *The Papers of the Bibliographical Society of America*, Vol. 99, No. 4 (December 2005): pp. 505–538.

Kerr, Cecil. *The Life of the Venerable Philip Howard, Earl of Arundel and Surrey*. London: Longmans, 1926.

Pollen, John Hungerford, S.J., and William MacMahon, S.J., eds. *Ven. Philip Howard, Earl of Arundel 1557–1595*. English Martrys, Vol. 2. London: Catholic Record Society, 1919.

The Poetry of Venerable Philip Howard

‡ ‡ ‡

A Hymn

WHEREIN THE PRAISES OF ALL CREATURES ARE OFFERED UP UNTO THE CREATOR

(*Written in the Tower of London*)

Oh Christ, the glorious crown
Of virgins that are pure;
Who dost a love and thirst for thee
Within their minds procure;
Thou are the spouse of those
That chaste and humble be,
The hope, the life, the only help
Of such as trust in thee.
All charity of those
Whose souls thy love doth warm;
All simple pleasures of such minds
As think no kind of harm;
All sweet delights wherewith
The patient hearts abound,
Do blaze thy name, and with thy praise
They make the world resound.
The sky, the land, the sea,
And all on earth below,
The glory of thy worthy Name
Do with their praises show.
The winter yields thee praise,
And summer doth the same,
The sun, the moon, the stars and all
Do magnify thy name.

The roses that appear
So fair to outward sight;
The violets with their scent
Do yield so great delight;
The pearls, the precious stones,
The birds, thy praise do sing,
The woods, the wells, and all delights,
Which from this earth do spring.
What creature, Oh sweet Lord,
From praising thee can stay?
What earthly thing but, filled with joy,
Thine honor doth bewray[1]?
Let us, therefore, with praise
Thy mighty works express,
With heart and hand, with mind, and all
Which we from thee possess.

1. "Bewray" meaning *make known.*

Meditation upon Heaven
(*Written after his attainder*)

No eye hath seen what joys the Saints obtain,
No ear hath heard what comforts are possessed;
No heart can think in what delight they reign
Nor pen express their happy port of rest,
Where pleasure flows, and grief is never seen,
Where good abounds and ill is banish'd clean.
Those sacred saints remain in perfect peace,
Which Christ confessed, and walked in his ways,
They shine in bliss, which now can never cease,
And to his name do sing eternal praise:
Before his throne in white they ever stand,
And carry palms of triumph in their hand.
Above them all the Virgin hath a place,
Which caused the world with comfort to abound;
The beams do shine in her unspotted face,
And with the stars her head is richly crowned:
In glory she all creatures passeth far,
The moon her shoes, the sun her garments are.
Lo, here the look which angels do admire!
Lo, here the spring from which all goodness flows!
Lo, here that sight which men and saints desire!
Lo, here that stalk on which our comfort grows!
Lo, this is she whom heaven and earth embrace,
Whom God did choose, and filled full of grace.
Next above her, and on a higher throne,
Our Savior in his manhood sitteth here;
From whom proceeds all perfect joy alone,
And in whose face all glory doth appear:
The saints' delight conceived cannot be
When they a man the Lord of angels see.
Oh worthy place, where such a Lord is chief!

Oh glorious Lord who princely servants keeps,
Oh happy saints, which never taste of grief!
Oh blessed state, where malice ever sleeps!
No one is here of base or mean degree,
But all are known the sons of God to be!

A Fourfold Meditation

OF THE FOUR LAST THINGS: OF THE HOUR OF DEATH, DAY OF JUDGMENT, PAINS OF HELL AND JOYS OF HEAVEN[2]

OF THE HOUR OF DEATH

1 Oh wretched man, which lovest earthly things
And to this world hast made thyself in thrall,
Whose short delights eternal sorrow brings,
Whose sweet in show in truth is bitter gall:
Whose pleasures fade ere scarce they be possessed,
And grieve him least that most do them detest.

2 Thou art not sure one moment for to live,
And at thy death thou leavest all behind,
Thy lands and goods no succor then can give,
Thy pleasures past are crosses, to thy mind:
Thy friend the world can yield thee no release,
Thy greatest joy will prove thy greatest grief.

3 The time will come when Death will thee assault:
Conceive it then as present for to be,
That thou in time mayest seek to mend thy fault,
And in thy life thine errors plainly see:
Imagine now thy course is almost spent,
And mark thy friends how deeply they lament.

4 Thy wife doth howl and pierce the very skies,
Thy children's tears their sorrows doth bewray,[3]

2. **Editor's Note:** In the original edition of *Lyra Martyrum*, "A Fourfold Meditation" was attributed to Robert Southwell, but recent scholarship has shown it likely to be the work of Philip Howard.

3. "Bewray," meaning *make known* or *divulge*.

Thy kinsfolk mourn and weep with woeful cries,
Now thou must die and can'st no longer stay:
Lo! here the joys and treasures of thy heart:
Thy race is run: from them thou must depart.

5 With pain thou dost lie, gasping all for breath,
Past hope of life or hope of any good;
Thy present state a lively form of death,
Thy heart become all cold for want of blood:
Thy nostrils run and gasping thou dost lie,
Thy loathsome sight thy friends begin to fly.

6 Thy voice doth yield a hoarse and hollow sound,
Thy dying head doth greedy seems to sleep;
Thy senses all with horror doth abound,
Thy feet doth die and death doth upward creep:
Thy eyes doth stand, fast set into thine head,
Thy jaws doth fall and show thee almost dead.

7 What dost thou think, now all thy senses fail?
What dost thou say by pleasure here is won?
How dost thou now thy passed life bewail?
How dost thou wish, thy course were new to run?
What wouldst thou do thy ending life to save?
What wouldst thou give for that thou canst not have?

8 Thy body now must from the soul depart,
Thy lands and goods another must possess,
Thy joys are past on which thou settest thine heart,
Thy pains to come no creature can express;
Lo here the fruit and gain of all thy sin,
Thy life must end and death must now begin.

9 Thy former faults are set before thine eyes
And monstrous shows which seemed before so small,
To swallow thee, Despair in secret lies
And all thy sins with terror thee appall:
With scalding sighs they make thee now to moan,
And in thy soul with sorrow thou dost groan.

10 Thou wailest now the pleasing of thy will,
Thy evil-got goods doth make thee so lament,
Thy vain delights with anguish thee doth fill,
Thy wanton tricks thy conscience doth torment:
Thy sweetest sins doth bring thee bitter smart,
Thy heinous faults oppress thy dying heart.

11 With dreadful fear they shake thy doleful mind
And bent to fight, with force they thee enclose,
In worldly help no rescue thou canst find,
And standing now amidst thy mortal foes,
A thousand deaths would seem a lesser pain,
Then this estate in which thou dost remain.

12 No tongue, no pen, nor creature can bewray
How all thy sins their festered rancor show,
How dreadful sights with sorrow thee dismay,
How blust'ring storms of griefs begin to blow.
Thy joys are gone, which were thy God before,
Thy life is done and shall return no more.

13 What booteth it thy lewdness to repent
And leave to sin when sin forsaketh thee?
What canst thou do when all thy force is spent?
Will then our Lord with this appeased be?
Thy life thou led'st in service of his foe
And servest him when life thou must forgo.

14 Now heaven to win no pains thou wouldst refuse,
Nor spare thy goods to ease thy woeful state,
Of all thy sins thou dost thyself accuse
And call for grace when calling comes too late:
For sin thou didst while life and power did last,
And leavest now, when force to sin is past.

15 "Then had—I—wist...", with sorrow thou dost say,
But after-wits repentance ever breed,
The day is come, thy debt thou now must pay
And yield to death, when life thou most shalt need:
Thy breath is stopped in twinkling of an eye,
Thy body dead in ugly form doth lie.

16 Thy carcass now like carrion men doth shun,
Thy friends do haste thy burial to procure,
Thy servants seek from thee away to run,
Thy loathsome stench no creature can endure:
And they which took in thee their most delight,
Do hate thee most and most abhor thy sight.

17 Thy flesh shall serve for maggots for a prey,
For pampering which both sea and land was sought,
Thy body must transformed be to clay,
For whose delight such costly clothes were bought:
Thy pride in dust, thy glory in the grave,
Thy flesh in earth their ending now shall have.

18 Behold! The place in which thou dost abide
Is loathsome, dark, unsweet, and very straight:
With rotten bones beset on every side
And crawling worms to feed on thee doth wait.
Oh hard exchange! Oh vile and hateful place!
Where earth and filth thy carcass must embrace.

19 Oh wretched state! Oh most unhappy man!
Yet were it well if nothing were behind,
If all might end as here it first began,
Some comfort were such ending for to find:
For then as God of nothing thee did frame,
By course again thou shouldst become the same.

20 But live thou must, a thousand deaths to die,
And dying still, yet never wholly dead;
Thou must appear before the Judge on high,
And have reward as thou thy life hast lead:
Thy time is come, thou canst no longer stay:
The judge is set and bootless is delay.

OF THE DAY OF JUDGMENT

21 Behold his power. Lo whom thou didst offend,
For vain delights, which were but mere deceit;
Behold on him how Angels doth attend,
And all that court do for his coming wait:
Behold his throne of glory in the skies,
And see how wrath doth sparkle for his eyes.

22 Lo this is he who everything did make,
Whom Heaven and Earth do praise both night and day;
Lo here the look at which the Angels quake,
Lo here the Lord whom all things doth obey:
His will is law and may not be withstand,
His wrath consumes and killeth out of hand.

23 Oh filthy soul, how may this wrath be born?
Or can a worm his fury now abide?
The Angels laugh thy filthiness to scorn,

They hate thy sin and thee for swelling pride:
They shine with beams far brighter than the Sun,
And call on God that Justice may be done.

24 Each creature cries that punished thou may'st be,
Whom in thy life thou lewdly didst abuse;
Both Heaven and Earth are foes protest to thee
And all thy thoughts of sin doth thee accuse:
Thy words and deeds against thee now are brought,
And all thy filth which sin in thee hath wrought.

25 Thou cited art a just account to show,
How far thou sought thy self for to deny,
How all thy lands and wealth thou didst bestow
And with thy goods thy brothers want supply:
What care thou hadst, thy maker's name to praise,
What pain thou takest to walk in all his ways.

26 The Judge doth ask how all thy life was spent,
If from offence thy senses thou didst keep;
If in thy soul thou truly didst repent
And for thy sin with hearty sorrow weep:
If thou his fear didst set before thine eyes,
And for his love all worldly joys despise.

27 If eke thy foes revenge thou hast not wrought,
If to thy friends thou never were unkind;
If earthly pomp thou ever set at naught,
If secret hate thou hast not kept in mind:
If thou alike didst joy and sorrow take
And with thy heart all carnal lust forsake.

28 Thy thought and words the Judge doth open lay,
And asketh now a straight account of all;

How thou didst here his motions obey,
  And for his grace with earnest fervor call:
    If all thy life on earth thou ledst upright,
    And in his love didst set thy whole delight.

29 What canst thou plead thy lewdness to excuse?
  When truth shall prove in all thou didst offend?
The Judge is just, thou mayst not him refuse,
  Thy cause is naught, thou canst not it defend:
    To hope for help, alas! it is in vain,
    The time is past, no help thou canst obtain.

30 Our Lord doth say, "How couldst thou use me so,
  Since I to thee both soul and body gave?
How durst thou seek and serve my mortal foe,
  Since I did die thy self from death to save?
    I gave thee all and me thou didst detest,
    He gave thee naught, yet wholly thee possessed.

31 "Thy lands and life did from my goodness flow,
  Thy flesh and bones I did of nothing frame;
Both wealth and wit I did on thee bestow,
  And gave thee all to praise my holy name:
    Yet with them all against me thou didst fight,
    And fled to them who bred me greatest spite.

32 "When I did speak thou seemest deaf and dumb,
  When he did call thou made him answer straight;
He never stayed but thou didst quickly come,
  And I without enforced was to wait:
    Oh thankless wretch thou me shalt see no more,
    But dwell with him who had thy heart before.

33 "Thou shalt with him for ever more remain,
To whom thy self for pleasure thou hast sold;
His will thou wrought'st and mine thou didst disdain,
His right thou art, I cannot thee withhold:
Thy own deserts have made thee his to be,
The choice was thine, no wrong is done to thee."

34 Then comes the Devil and to our Lord doth say,
"Oh righteous Judge, this wretch I ought to have;
For in his life he would not thee obey,
But with his heart to me himself he gave:
My precepts eke he practiced day and night,
And me to please he made his whole delight.

35 "Himself he vowed to serve me all his days,
His eyes were fixed upon my counsel still;
His feet were bent to walk in all my ways,
His heart was set for to perform my will:
His life and lands I drew him on to spend,
To doing that which might thee most offend.

36 "He scorned thy power and quite refused thy grace,
Thy bitter pains—he banished from his eyes;
Thy precious blood he never would embrace.
Thy gracious wounds he lewdly did despise:
Thy threats for sin he reckoned as a jest,
Thy words and will in all he did detest.

37 "Thy glorious death he seemed to disdain,
And followed that in which he did delight;
For serving thee he took not any pain,
But all thy love with hate he did requite:
What reason then thy glory should he see,
Of which he seemed so careless for to be.

38 “Thou didst him make and on him all bestow,
I nothing gave nor him to being brought;
Yet thee he left, to whom he love did owe,
And me he served who never gave him ought:
What wouldst thou more thou usest not to wrong,
And he to me in Justice doth belong.”

39 Behold, Oh soul! How God doth thee refuse,
And how his foe doth claim thee as his own;
Thy conscience doth with horror thee accuse
And reap, thou must as thou before hast sown:
The Lord of Lords doth thee condemn to lie
In endless flames where living thou shalt die.

40 Oh wretched soul! What shall become of thee?
What greater pain can any heart devise?
Yet worse there is, if worse there yet may be,
Thy body must to Judgment shortly rise:
And both alike in Hell must suffer smart,
As both in earth in sin had equal part.

41 All sinners fain would shun this dreadful day,
And wish it were without their peril passed;
The fear alone must needs their hearts dismay,
The sign appears and on it cometh fast:
Behold the Sun is dark which shined bright,
The stars do fall, the moon hath lost her light.

42 Behold how men are withered quite with woe,
And cannot find a harbor now of rest;
Behold on earth how senseless they do go,
Their faces pale, their hearts with fear oppressed:
Behold each where how beasts for terror cry,
And mark how men already seem to die.

43 Behold how blood the trees and branches sweat,
And how each thing in trembling wise doth quake;
Behold the sea against the land doth beat,
And roaring loud doth force the earth to shake:
Her surges mount, her swellings fair shows,
And on the land her fish with rage she throws.

44 The clouds like smoke do thicken in the skies,
The mountains move, the earth doth open wide;
The blustering winds with storms and tempests,
The stoutest hearts their faces seek to hide:
Both rich and poor from cities now are fled,
And all in caves do run to shroud their head.

45 Each living thing for help doth cry and call,
And savage beasts unto the city fly;
The earth doth quake, the strongest towers fall,
And beasts remain where men did use to lie:
The course begins of nature here to fail,
The heavens doth mourn and all things else doth wail.

46 The angels loud their trumpets dreadful sound,
And summons all that ever life possessed;
The Earth with woe and terror doth abound,
The dead arise that long had been at rest:
Both quick and dead assembled round do stand,
And wait his will whose coming is at hand.

47 Behold how low both Heaven and Earth do bow,
And prostrate all his favor to desire;
Behold how Christ in glory cometh now,
And in the air appears a flame of fire:
The Earth for fear do tremble at this sight,
The sea is dried, the hills are molten quite.

48 The hardest rocks are turned into dust,
His furious wrath no creature can abide.
Their pains were sweet which now are proved just,
And need not seek in corners them to hide:
Our Lord rewards as merit he doth find,
Thrice happy they that bear a guiltless mind.

49 Oh cursed soul! How art thou drowned in care,
When all this sight is set before thine eyes;
Thy passing fear nor writhing can declare,
Thy body dark like Death do seem to rise:
Thy hope is past for easing of thy smart,
Thy sins are pricks to wound thy dying heart.

50 Behold how thou no favor here canst get,
Nor from thy foes by any means escape;
Thy right hand is with all thy sins beset,
Beneath thee Hell to swallow thee doth gape:
The fearful fiends upon thy left hand frown,
And lie in wait, to throw thee headlong down.

51 Above thee sits the Judge all filled with rage,
Whom in thy life thou lewdly didst offend;
No help thou hast his fury to assuage,
His brows he doth with anger fiercely bend:
And all the sins of men he doth repeat,
Which forceth now his fury to be great.

52 Within thee gnaws thy conscience void of grace,
And all the evil to which thou didst consent;
Without thee stands thy friends which wail thy case,
And do thy state with bitter grief lament:
On every side the world doth thee affright,
Whose terror shows, with flames that burneth bright.

53 If forward now thou tookest on thy way,
Thou headlong dost unto thy ruin run;
The devils do watch thy going back to stay,
No means is left misfortune for to shun:
What wilt thou do, environed thus with woe?
For neither back nor forward thou canst go.

54 Oh wretched man! How heavy is thy heart,
How dost thou wish for that which cannot be;
How dost thou sigh and quake in every part,
And must thy friends be severed thus from thee:
They filled with joy in glory now shall reign,
And full of grief thou torment must sustain.

55 The Judge's words are like a burning fire,
Which wasteth all it cometh to embrace;
It booteth not his mercy to require,
The time is past of calling now for grace:
Behold the Judge doth thee condemn to hell,
Where thou in pain for sin shalt ever dwell.

56 Oh doleful words! Oh most unhappy wight!
Thy head to shroud for mountains thou dost call;
Thy future pains are present in thy sight,
And cursed now the causes of thy fall:
Thy birth and life too late thou dost repent,
Yet wailest both and both in vain lament.

OF THE PAINS OF HELL

57 What tongue, what pen, what creature can express,
Those deadly griefs which always thou dost taste?
The longer time the comfort is the less,

Thy hope decays, thy sorrows never waste.
Oh bitter sweet that earthly pleasures breed!
Thy living death all torments doth exceed.

58 Thy wanton eyes those hellish monsters see,
Whose bloody minds thy ruin did conspire,
Whose sneezing seem like lightning for to be,
Whose monstrous mouths do cast out flames of fire:
Whose nostrils smoke, whose eyes are glowing red,
Whose whole delight by others smart is bred,

59 Thy wretched ears, which harkened unto lies,
Do hear how fiends do rage with all despite;
No noise is there but shrieks and hideous cries,
Which able are the stoutest heart to fright:
Where some blaspheme and some their states bewail,
Where others curse and never cease to rail.

60 Thy dainty nose, which had perfumes each day,
A loathsome stench forever must abide;
Which riseth up from damned bodies aye.
That heaped there do lie on every side:
Lo here the sweet thy smelling to content,
No worldly filth can yield so foul a scent.

61 Thy curious taste doth hunger there sustain,
Which did in meats such rare devices crave;
With burning thirst thou sufferest grievous pain,
And it to cool no water thou canst have:
No drop is there thy thirsting for to ease,
No hope of help that may thy grief appease.

62 Thy feeling yet the greatest pain doth bear,
With fiery flames which all thy parts torment;

An extreme cold thou also findest there,
With gnashing teeth that makes thee to lament:
Thy tears with heat in streams are daily shed,
Thy teeth for cold do chatter in thy head.

63 If for a while no creature can endure,
In earthly fire, one member for to be;
What torments do thy passed joys procure,
In endless flames thy members all to see!
What grief, what pain, what sorrows do they breed,
Which earthly flames in all do far exceed!

64 The devils with flouts do laugh thee now to scorn,
Thy flesh and bones in sunder they do tear;
Thy cursed skin with cruel whips is worn,
Thy woeful heart is filled full with fear:
With inward woe thy soul is sore oppressed,
With outward pain thy body finds no rest.

65 Thy torments strange do breed thee bitter grief,
And rest in thine imagination still;
Thine own conceit which now should yield release,
Doth labor more with sorrow thee to fill:
Thou thinkest most what most thou wouldst eschew,
Thy grief thy thoughts and thoughts thy grief renew.

66 Thy memory doth call unto thy mind,
The short delight of all thy pleasures past;
It wounds thy heart these pains for them to find,
Which grievous are and shall for ever last:
Thy desperate case no comfort can obtain,
Thy passed joys increase thy present pain.

67 Thine understanding doth thy misery show,
And telleth thee thou art in Satan's jaws;
For short delights, thy loss it makes thee know,
And in thy soul the worm of conscience gnaws:
Those fading joys in rage thou dost defy,
And in despite they make thee thus to cry:

68 "My former joy a shadow was in deed,
It did not last, but passed quick away;
My present pain all measure doth exceed,
No wit nor art my torments can bewray:
A time there was when bliss I might have won,
But time is past and all my course is run.

69 "Oh cursed time, in which I time forsook,
A little pain had rid me of my woe!
Oh cursed joys in which I pleasure took,
For pleasing you all pleasures I forgo!
And here in hell each kind of pain I find,
Which wastes my flesh and wounds my woeful mind.

70 "If I my sins with sorrow had confessed,
They had to me been clean remitted all;
Instead of grief, I glory had possessed,
If I for grace had bent my mind to call:
Oh wretched wretch, that for shall a pain,
Refusing bliss, in torment must remain.

71 "The greatest joys which do in earth abound,
Can in a world not yield so much delight;
As here by pain is in a moment found,
Whose biasing woe is present still in sight:
What fancy then bewitched my wretched heart,
For fained joys to suffer endless smart?

72 My parents were the causers of my woe,
And all the meat on which I ever fed;
My carnal friend hath proved my greatest foe,
And unto me this mischief now hath bred:
Accuse me all that hath my ruin wrought,
And every mean which me to being brought.

73 Thrice happy they on earth that never were!
Their state is blest that never came to life!
Oh blessed wombs that children never bare!
Oh happy breast which suck did never give!
Oh deadly pain! Oh most unhappy place!
Oh cursed wretch whom ill mishap embrace."

74 Lo, hear the plaints in this infernal lake,
Where scorpions sting and scourges thee torment;
Where hammers beat and devils a roaring make,
Where hope is past and damned souls lament:
Where worms do crawl and ugly serpents creep,
Where pains abound and sorrows make thee weep.

75 Against our Lord thou raisest with despite,
And him thou dost with raging words defy;
Thou barred art from seeing any light,
And while ye live thou must forever die:
Lo here the fruit which worldly pleasures bring,
Thy pains agree in measure with thy sin.

76 Thy sweet delights are come to woe and wrack,
Thy happy state unto a wretched case;
Thy greedy mind is punished here with lack,
Thy lecherous arms do ugly fiends embrace:
Thy envious soul doth howl and deadly pain,
Thy haughty heart doth suffer deep disdain.

77 Thou findest smart instead of pleasant games,
Thy dainty wines are turned to bitter gall;
Thy costly clothes are now made burning flames,
Thy lofty pride hath now a loathsome fall:
Thou nothing dost which may afford thee ease,
But feelest all which may thee most displease.

78 Yet chiefly one which far doth all exceed,
And as it is none rightly can esteem;
It grieves thee most and makes thy heart to bleed,
And joined with it the other nothing seem:
Then judge what pain this torture brings to thee,
When match to it all nothing seems to be.

79 Thy senses feel for every sin a pain,
So rated there as here thou took'st delight;
And now for that our Lord doth thee disdain,
Thou banished art for ever from his sight:
The pain of sense small torment thou dost find,
When thou this loss dost call unto thy mind.

80 A grievous loss which cannot be expressed!
Oh cause of grief and spring of deadly woe;
The soul hath lost the center of her rest,
Thy hope, thy help, thy life thou must forgo:
No pain or loss with this may be compared,
It passeth all and cannot be declared.

81 From hope of joy this is an endless bar,
And greatest plague that God on sin bestows;
Compared with this thy tortures pleasant are,
And all thy loss an easy burthen shows:
Thy bitterest pains are trifles in thine eyes,
Thy burning flames thou seemest to despise.

82 What woe, what smart, what pain can be expressed,
Which waiteth now on thee for to be laid!
With swords of grey thy head is daily pressed,
With dreadful fear thy senses are dismayed:
Thy eye hath lost what most she did desire,
Thy body burns in flames of endless fire.

83 And if thy pains an ending might obtain,
When years there were of many thousands run;
As on the earth have lighten drops of rain,
Since first of all this wretched world begun:
Some help this hope might bring unto thy mind,
When hope were left an end at last to find.

84 But of them all no ease nor end thou hast,
Within thy soul some comfort might procure;
No time will help thy sorrows for to waste,
While God is God thy torture shall endure:
Thy pain in truth is more than can be told,
The sight in thought no creature can unfold.

85 Oh dying life! Oh sea of endless smart!
Which nature hates and all things else detest;
Oh living death, no life or death thou art,
For death hath end and life hath sometime rest:
The worst of both our Lord hath put in thee,
That neither nor end might other be.

86 Oh damned soul! How dost thou roar and cry!
What deadly griefs thee daily do oppress!
But lift a while thy cursed eyes on high,
And see what joys the blessed there possess
That by the sight, thy torment may increase
And for thy loss thy sorrows never cease.

OF THE JOYS OF HEAVEN

87 And first behold the beauty of the place
Where all the saints with Christ in glory reign;
Where honor is not mixed with disgrace,
Where joy is free from talk of any pain:
Where great rewards attend on good deserts,
And all delights possesseth faithful hearts

88 Oh wicked wretch! This city now behold,
Which doth surpass the reach of any thought;
The gates are pearl, the streets are finest gold
With precious stones the walls are wholly wrought:
Of sun and moon it needeth not the light,
For ever there the Lamb is shining bright

89 And from his seat a crystal river flows,
Where life doth run and pleasure ever springs;
On every side a tree of comfort grows,
Which saving help to every nation brings:
It worketh rest and stinteth worldly strife,
It flieth death and bringeth endless life.

90 This goodly place all beauty doth surmount
And all this world in largeness passeth far
The earth itself in bigness in account
Not equal is unto the smallest star
Oh worthy place whose glory doth excel,
Thrice happy they that there attains to dwell!

91 No saint there is but brighter seems to be
Than sun or moon, whose beauties wonders breed;
What glory then so many saints to see,
Which all the stars in number far exceed!

All glorious there where glory doth abound,
Oh blessed state where bliss is ever found.

92 Archangels are but underservants there,
And angels do their maker's will obey;
The powers in joy with triumph do appear,
The beauties shine, the thrones their beams display:
The cherubims do yield a famous light,
The seraphims with love are burning, shining bright.

93 Here Patriarchs have their joy for all their pain,
The Prophets eke with endless glory blest;
The Martyrs do a worthy crown obtain,
The Virgins find a haven of happy rest:
To all their joys in glory they are met,
And now possess what long they sought to get.

94 Those sacred saints remain in perfect peace,
Which Christ confessed and walked in his ways;
They swim in bliss which now shall never cease
And singing all, his name for ever praise:
Before his throne in white they daily stand,
And carry palms of triumph in their hands.

95 The angels then are next in their degree,
Whose order is in number to be nine;
No heart can think what joy it is to see,
How all those troupes with lamps in glory shine:
The joy is more than writing can express,
Oh happy eyes that may these joys possess.

96 Above them all the Virgin hath a place,
Which caused the world with comfort to abound;
And beams do shine in her unspotted face,

And with the stars her head is richly crowned:
In glory she all creatures passeth far,
The moon her shoes, the sun her garments are.

97 Oh Queen of Heaven! Oh pure and glorious sight!
Most blessed thou above all women art!
This city drunk thou makest with delight,
And with thy beams rejoiceth every heart:
Our bliss was lost and it thou didst restore,
The angels all and men do thee adore.

98 Lo! here the look which Angels do admire!
Lo! here the spring from whom all goodness flows!
Lo! here the sight that men and saints desire!
Lo! here the stalks on which our comfort grows!
Lo this is she whom heaven and earth embrace,
Whom God did choose and filled full of grace.

99 And next to her, but in a higher throne,
Our Savior in his manhood sitteth here;
From whom proceeds all perfect joy alone,
And in whose face all glory doth appear:
The saints' delight conceived cannot be,
When they a man the Lord of angels see.

100 They ravished are with joy in seeing this,
How Christ our Lord the highest place obtains;
They now behold the seat of endless bliss,
And joy to mark how he in triumph reigns:
What joy to men moreover can befall,
Then here to see a man the Lord of all?

101 More joy it yields than any can devise,
A greater bliss than may in words be told;

His piercing beams doth dazzle all their eyes,
His brightness scarce his angels can behold:
The saints in him their wished comfort finds,
And now enjoy what most content their minds.

102 To think on this it passeth human wit,
The more we think the less we come to know;
He doth upon his Father's right hand sit,
And all the saints their humble service show:
His sight to them doth endless comfort bring,
And they to him all praises ever sing.

103 Oh worthy place, where such a Lord is chief!
Oh glorious Lord, which princely servants keeps!
Oh happy saints, which never taste of grief!
Oh blessed state, where malice ever sleeps!
No one is here of base or mean degree,
But all are known the sons of God to be.

104 What higher place can any prince attain
Than son to him which ruleth all above?
Yet is their state not subject to disdain,
But in their minds like brethren they do love:
No place is left for any hate, or fear,
But here they all one heart and soul do bear.

105 Oh happy place, where discord never fights!
The joys of all are found in every breast;
For each as much in others joys delights,
As if alone it in himself did rest:
In all their joys no difference is there known,
For each accounts them all to be his own.

106 And those they taste wherewith their Lord abounds:
As part of theirs his glory do they take;
Unto themselves by union it redounds,
And all his joys their glory perfect make:
So fast are knit the members to the head,
As over them his joys are wholly spread.

107 What joy is best which here they do not find?
What greater bliss, what pleasure may be more?
What can by us conceiveth be in mind,
Which hath not been recited here before?
Yet one delight behind as yet remains
Which all in all and all in it contains.

108 They face to face do God Almighty see!
And all in him as in a perfect glass:
No good there is, but there is found to be,
And all delights this vision doth surpass.
Each sight doth yield the heart her perfect rest,
Because no good without him is possessed.

109 He present, past, and future things doth show,
And therefore rests their understanding here;
There nothing is but they in him do know,
And to their eyes all plainly doth appear:
They now obtain what long they sought to get,
And all their thoughts are on him wholly set.

110 Their will doth last in loving of his sight,
In which consists all good that can be thought;
She here hath fixed her love and whole delight,
And never will from loving this be brought:
For here all good and goodness doth abound,
And never can without this good be found.

111 Their whole Desire from hence doth never part,
  But settled here forever doth abide;
This sight doth fill the mouth of every heart,
  And nothing leaves for them to wish beside:
    Without desire, content they still remain,
    And here Desire with full delight obtain.

112 Their Faith beholds her best beloved guest,
  And her belief this sight doth here fulfil;
Their constant Hope her hope hath now possessed,
  And him enjoys for whom she hoped still:
    Their Charity, not perfect full before,
    To perfect state this vision doth restore.

113 Oh glorious sight! Oh sum of endless bliss!
  Which never wanes, nor seemeth for to waste!
Who ever saw so fair a sight as this,
  Who ever did such heaps of comfort taste?
    What can be thought that cannot here be had?
    Where all doth joy and none are ever sad?

114 They here possess what may content them most,
  And nothing want that perfect bliss may bring;
With all delight here breathes the Holy Ghost,
  Which always makes a fresh and endless spring:
    No day is here, no morning, noon, nor night,
    But ever one and always shining bright.

115 Oh blessed joys, which all the souls possess!
  Oh happy fruit, that virtue here hath won!
And in degrees the bodies find no less,
  But shine with beams far brighter than the sun:
    Nor subject now to sickness, grief, or pain,
    But glorious all, immortal they remain.

116 And proper joys each sense in private finds,
Their eyes behold that passing glorious sight;
Where nothing wants for to content their minds,
And all things else which may them most delight:
Their ears are fed with hearing of sweet sounds,
And them to please all music here abounds.

117 From songs of praise the saints no moment spare,
No tears are seen nor any there do weep;
But in this place the music is so rare,
As half a sound would bring all hearts asleep.
And every sense a proper pleasure takes,
Which joined in one, their glory perfect makes.

118 No eye hath seen what joys the saints obtain,
Nor ear hath heard what comforts are possessed;
No heart can think in what delight they reign,
Nor pen express their happy port of rest:
Where pleasure flows and grief is never seen,
Where good abounds and ill is banished clean.

119 And of those joys no creature end shall see,
The longer time the sweeter they do show;
While God endures they cannot ended be,
And never waste but always seem to grow:
When worlds are worn and millions many passed,
They now begin and shall forever last.

120 Oh state of joy, when endless joy remains,
Oh haven of bliss, where none doth suffer wrack!
Oh happy house, which all delight contains!
Oh blessed state, which never feeleth lack!
Oh goodly tree, which fruit doth ever bear!
Oh quiet state, which danger need not fear!

121 Oh mixture pure, which basest dross refines!
Oh pleasant place, which only comfort brings!
Oh joyful sun, where glory ever shines!
Oh fruitful soil, where pleasure ever springs!
Oh glorious souls! Oh bodies wholly blessed!
Oh sea of good and of all good the best.

122 Oh damned wretch! The thought of this alone
Oppresseth thee with heaps of deadly care;
And sighing now in spirit thou dost groan,
When with their bliss thy woe thou dost compare:
Thy grievous loss doth grieve thy wretched heart,
And it with grief redoubles all thy smart.

123 If all the world by conquest thou hadst won,
A trifle now thou thinkest all to give;
That on the earth thy race were now to run,
And thou again were suffered here to live:
Another course thou wouldst resolve to take,
And serving God thy carnal will forsake.

124 The straightest life thou wouldst no pain esteem,
Thy praying would a passing joy appear;
Thy fasting oft no trouble then would seem,
Nor any grief, the hardest penance here:
A joy thou wouldst account the sharpest pain,
To scape from Hell and endless bliss obtain.

125 Now must I call, Oh worldly man! to thee,
The end where first I did begin to write;
That all these joys and pains which thou dost see
May move thy mind to lead thy life aright:
Thy heart will melt to think upon thy case
If there be left but half a spark of grace.

126 Thou findest here what thou wilt wish at last,
And that account which none can ever shun;
Then frame thy life before thy time be past,
As thou wilt wish that thou in time hadst done:
Lest thou in vain doth wail thy wretched state,
When time is past and wailing comes too late.

BLESSED HENRY WALPOLE, S.J.

(1558–APRIL 17, 1595)

HENRY WALPOLE'S LIFE demonstrates the immediate, transforming influence that the Elizabethan Catholic martyrs had upon their contemporaries. Walpole was born into a large family with Catholic leanings (he was the oldest of ten children) and regularly associated with recusants; nevertheless, he followed an unexceptional path in education and vocational training in law, until he attended the public disputations that the English government staged in the Tower of London for the captured Jesuit Edmund Campion. Campion famously defended himself and the Catholic position so well that those who watched were deeply moved by his cause, and Walpole was no exception. He attended Campion's trial and his execution. Indeed, Walpole stood so close to the scaffold upon which Campion was dismembered that he was splattered with the martyr's blood. This proved to be like an indelible mark for Walpole; he resolved to take upon himself the labor that Campion had begun.

Walpole immediately set about writing his poem "Upon the Death of M. Edmund Campion," included here (p. 95), and the poem quickly became popular. Catholics copied the poem and passed it around their circles, and one of Walpole's friends, who had a private printing press, soon set it in type. The popularity of the poem is a testament to Edmund Campion's great influence, and is a fine example of the way that the persecuted Catholics turned to poetry for comfort, to strengthen their own resolve, and to memorialize their executed companions. The government had been deeply frustrated in its plans to make an example of Campion, since he had proved so able in his defense, and so winning in his bearing and character, and the popularity of Walpole's poem was an unacceptable continuation of Campion's influence. The government sought to destroy all copies of the poem, and the man who had printed it had his ears cut off as a punishment. When Elizabeth's government began to suspect that Walpole was the poem's author, he fled England, and joined the English College in Rheims in July of 1582.

After ten months studying theology in Rheims, Walpole made his way to Rome, where he studied at the English College until he was accepted into the Jesuit order. He was ordained in 1588, and in the years that followed, three of his younger brothers and one of his cousins followed in his footsteps, all joining the Society of Jesus. After his ordination, Walpole was assigned to serve as the Chaplain to Catholic forces in the Netherlands, and in 1589 he was captured and tortured when English troops took the town of Flushing. One of his younger brothers found that he was prisoner in the Netherlands, and managed to pay his ransom before he was transported to England. Following this, in 1592, he was assigned to assist Robert Persons in founding the Jesuit College in Seville, Spain. Persons had been Edmund Campion's companion in that first mission to England that had so transformed Walpole's life. His work in Spain, however, was short-lived. Walpole had long made known his desire to follow Campion's path and return to England, and in 1593 the Jesuits agreed to send him on the next mission.

If Walpole had been fortunate to escape when captured in Flushing, he was distinctly unfortunate in his efforts to enter England. Owing to his poem about Campion he was a known and hated figure to the English government, and spies reported his return to the kingdom. During his crossing, terrible weather forced his ship to land in Yorkshire rather than Norfolk, a wholly unfamiliar area where he had no definite connections. The authorities quickly hunted him down, capturing him on December 7, 1593, and sending him to York Castle. Walpole readily admitted he was a Jesuit, but insisted upon his loyalty to the Queen, and refused to divulge the names of his Catholic connections. Notably, just as had happened with Edmund Campion, the government arranged for several disputations with Anglican divines, and despite the hostile situation, Walpole was praised for his zeal and learning. Frustrated by their inability to get more information from him, Walpole was sent to London to be tortured by the brutal Richard Topcliffe, an infamously vicious man who had a rack installed in his house, and who had tortured many Catholics, including Robert Southwell. Indeed, when Walpole was sent to the Tower of London, both Southwell and Philip Howard were imprisoned there at the same time, though Walpole was kept in solitary confinement and did not meet them.

Topcliffe tortured Henry Walpole terribly, putting him on the rack repeatedly, and Walpole did eventually offer the names of some Catholics who were in seminaries in Spain. Yet, he never surrendered any information about Catholics in England, despite Topcliffe's best efforts, and he was finally sent back to York for trial in 1595. He was quickly found guilty of being a priest, and was executed on April 17, 1595, with particular bitterness and brutality: While he knelt to say his final prayers, he was suddenly pushed off the scaffold, then immediately drawn and quartered.

Sources and Further Reading

Jessopp, Augustus. *One Generation of a Norfolk House*. 2nd ed. London: Burns and Oates, 1879.

Ryan, Anthony Charles. "Walpole, Henry [St. Henry Walpole] (bap. 1558, d. 1595)." In *Oxford Dictionary of National Biography*. New York: Oxford University Press, 2004.

The Poetry of Blessed Henry Walpole, S.J

‡ ‡ ‡

Upon the Death of M. Edmund Campion One of the Society of the Holy Name of Jesus

Why do I use my paper, ink, and pen,
And call my wits to counsel what to say?
Such memories were made for mortal men,
I speak of saints whose names cannot decay:
An angel's trump were fitter for to sound
Their glorious death, if such on earth were found.

Pardon my want, I offer naught but will,
Their register remaineth safe above.
Campion exceeds the compass of my skill,
Yet let me use the measure of my love,
And give me leave in low and homely verse,
His high attempts in England to rehearse.

He came by vow: the cause, to conquer sin,
His armor prayer: the word his targe and shield,
His comfort heaven: his spoil our souls to win,
The devil his foe, the wicked world the field,
His triumph joy, his wage eternal bliss,
His captain Christ, which ever blessed is.

From ease to pain, from honor to disgrace,
From love to hate, to danger being well,
From safe abode to fears in every place,
Contemning death to save our souls from hell,

Our new Apostle coming to restore
The faith which Austin[1] planted here before.

His nature's flowers were mixed with herbs of grace,
His mild behavior tempered well with skill,
A lowly mind possessed a learned place,
A sugared speech, a rare and virtuous will.
A saint-like man was set on earth below,
The seed of truth in erring hearts to sow.

With tongue and pen the truth he taught and wrote,
By force whereof they came to Christ apace.
But when it pleased God, it was his lot
He should be thralled, he lent him so much grace,
His patience then did work as much or more
As had his heavenly speeches done before.

His fare was hard, yet mild and sweet his cheer,
His prison close, yet free and loose his mind,
His torture great, yet small or none his fear,
His offers large, but nothing could him blind.
Oh constant man, Oh mind, Oh virtue strange,
Whom want, nor woe, nor fear, nor hope could change.

From rack in Tower they brought him to dispute,
Bookless, alone, to answer all that came,
Yet Christ gave grace, he did them all confute
So sweetly there in glory of his name,
That even the adverse part are forced to say
That Campion's cause did bear the bell away.

1. "Austin," meaning *Augustine* [*of Canterbury*].

This foil enraged the minds of some so far,
They thought it best to take his life away,
Because they saw he would their matter mar,
And leave them shortly naught at all to say:
Traitor he was with many and silly[2] slight,
Yet packed a jury that cried guilty straight.

Religion there was treason to the Queen,
Preaching of penance war against the land,
Priests were such dangerous men as have not been,
Prayers and beads were slight and force of hand,
Cases of conscience bane unto the state.
So blind is error, so false a witness hate.

And yet behold these lambs be drawn to die,
Treason proclaimed, the queen is put in fear,
Out upon Satan, fie malice, fie,
Speakest thou to them that did the guiltless hear?
Can humble souls departing now to Christ,
Protest untrue? Avaunt, foul fiend, thou liest.

My sovereign Liege, behold your subjects' end,
Your secret foes do misinform your Grace:
Who in your cause their holy lives would spend,
As traitors, die, a rare and monstrous case.
The bloody wolf condemns the harmless sheep
Before the dog, the while the shepherds sleep.

England look up, thy soil is stained with blood,
Thou hast made martyrs, many of thine own.
If thou hast grace their deaths will do thee good,
The seed will take, which in such blood is sown,

2. "Silly," meaning *innocent*.

And Campion's learning fertile so before,
Thus watered too, must needs of force be more.

‡ ‡ ‡

Remember you that would oppress the cause,
The Church is Christ's, his honor cannot die,
Though Hell herself revest[3] her gristly jaws,
And join in league with schism and heresy,
Though craft devise, and cruel rage oppress,
Yet skill will write and martyrdom confess.

You thought perhaps when learned Campion dies,
His pen must cease, his sugared tongue be still;
But you forgot how loud his death it cries
How far beyond the sound of tongue and quill.
You did not know how rare and great a good
It was to write his precious gifts in blood.

Living he spoke to them that present were,
His writings took their censure of the view,
Now fame reports his learning far and near,
And now his death confirms his doctrine true.
His virtues now are written in the skies,
And often read with holy inward eyes.

All Europe wonders at so rare a man,
England is filled with rumor of his end,
London must needs for it was present than
When constantly three saints their lives did spend.
The streets, the stones, the steps you haled them by,
Proclaim the cause for which these martyrs die.

---

3. "Revest," meaning *re-attire* or *clothe again*.

The Tower sayeth the truth he did defend,
The bar bears witness of his guiltless mind,
Tyburn doth tell he made a patient end,
On every gate his martyrdom we find,
In vain you wrought, that would obscure his name
For Heaven and Earth will still record the same.

Your sentence wrong pronounced of him here,
Exempts him from the judgment for to come;
Oh happy he that is not judged there!
God grant me, too, to have an earthly doom,
Your witness false and lewdly taken in,
Doth cause he is not now accused of sin.

His prison now the city of the King,
His rack and torture joys and heavenly bliss,
For men's reproach with angels doth he sing
A sacred song which everlasting is.
For shame but short and loss of small renown
He purchased hath an ever during crown.

His quartered limbs shall join with joy again,
And rise a body brighter than the sun,
Your blinded malice tortured him in vain,
For every wrench some glory hath him won,
And every drop of blood which he did spend,
Hath reaped a joy which never shall have end.

Can dreary death then daunt our faith, or pain?
Is't lingering life we fear to lose, or ease?
No, no, such death procureth life again,
'Tis only God we tremble to displease,
Who kills but once, and ever still we die,
Whose hot revenge torments eternally.

We cannot fear a mortal torment, we,
This martyr's blood hath moistened all our hearts,
Whose parted quarters when we chance to see,
We learn to play the constant Christian's parts.
His head doth speak, and heavenly precepts give,
How we that look should frame ourselves to live.

His youth instruct us how to spend our days,
His flying bids us how to banish sin,
His straight profession shows the narrow ways
Which they must walk that look to enter in.
His home return by danger and distress,
Emboldens us our conscience to profess.

His hurdle draws us with him to the cross,
His speeches there provoke us for to die,
His death doth say this life is but a loss,
His martyred blood from heaven to us doth cry,
His first and last and all conspire in this,
To show the way that leadeth unto bliss.

Blessed be God which lent him so much grace,
Thanked be Christ which blessed his martyrs so,
Happy is he which sees his master's face,
Cursed are they that thought to work him woe,
Bounden be we to give eternal praise,
To Jesus' name which such a man did raise.
Amen.

A Dialogue Between a Catholic and Consolation

CATHOLIC FIRST SPEAKETH

Is righteous Lot from sinful Sodom gone?
Is old Elias left alone again?
And hath the earth no just man, no not one,
The cause of Christ and Christians to sustain?
If holy life with true religion fail,
Then farewell faith, for falsehood will prevail.

CONSOLATION

No, Lot, thou hast some fellows in this land.
Elias, there are left seven thousand yet,
Rejoice thou earth, thou hast a warlike band
For our good Lord in martial order set,
By life and death this quarrel to begin
To vanquish falsehood, Satan, hell, and sin.

Although a worthy champion of your train
Were slain of late, and yet not vanquished,
Into his place another stepped again,
Whom Christ's spouse our common nurse hath bred.
Lament not then, for there are in his room
As good as he, expecting martyrdom.

CATHOLIC

Such men, no doubt, are very hard to find,

For dainty things are seldom sifted out;
The phoenix hath no partner of her kind;
A man perhaps may seek the world about,
Ere he may find one Campion again,
Wherefore his loss makes me the more complain.

Where shall you find so many gifts in one:
A wit so sharp, joined with such memory,
A great divine, hating promotion,
A lusty man possessing chastity,
A worthy imp sprung up of basest kind,
A learned man to bear a lowly mind?

Solon for pith, for wisdom Solomon,
Peter for style, and Paul for eloquence,
David for truth, for beauty Absolom,
For personage Saul, a Job for patience:
All that for which the fame of these began,
(A thing most strange) were joined in this one man.

Not rack, nor rope could daunt his dreadless mind,
No hope nor hap could move him where he stood,
He wrote the truth as in his books we find,
Which to confirm he sealed with his blood,
Which makes me doubt there are more such men.
Send workmen, Lord, into thy vineyard then.

CONSOLATION

Despair thou not, thou silly[4] mournful wight,
For there are more have took this match in hand.

4. "Silly," meaning *simple.*

We needs must win, our Lord himself doth fight,
The Canaanites shall be expulsed the land,
For Edmund lives and helpeth godly men
By prayers more than erst with tongue or pen.

His quarters hung on every gate do show,
His doctrine found through countries far and near,
His head set up so high doth call for moe
To fight the fight which he endured here,
The faith thus planted, thus restored must be.
Take up thy cross, saith Christ, and follow me.

As well as priests the laymen too shall frame
Their skill-less heads to take so good a vow,
God can of stones raise seed to Abraham,
Doubt not, therefore, for there will be enow.[5]

CATHOLIC

Fiat voluntas Dei[6] then say I,
We owe a death, and once we needs must die.

FINIS

5. "Enow," meaning *enough*.

6. "Fiat voluntas Dei," meaning *God's will be done*.

Hierusalem, Thy Joys Divine
A PRISONER'S SONG

Hierusalem, thy joys divine—
  No joys may be compared to them;
No people blessed so are thine
  No City like Hierusalem.

THE UNDER SONG

My thirsty soul desires her drought
  At heavenly fountains to refresh;
My prisoned mind would fain be out
  Of chains and fetters of the flesh.
She looketh up unto her state
  From whence she down by sin did slide;
She mourns the more the good she lost,
  For present ill she doth abide.

She longs, from rough and dangerous seas,
  To harbor in the haven of bliss,
Where safely anchored at her ease
  And shore of sweet contentment is.
From banishment she more and more
  Desires to see her country dear;
She sits and sends her sighs before
  Her joys and treasures all be there.

From Babylon she would return
  Unto her home and town of peace,
Hierusalem, where joys abound,
  Continue still and never cease.

There blustering winter never blows,
  Nor summer's parching heat doth harm;
It never freezes there nor snows;
  The weather ever temperate warm.

The trees do blossom, bud, and bear,
  The birds do ever chirp and sing,
The fruit is mellow all the year,
  They have an everlasting spring;
The pleasant gardens ever keep
  Their herbs and flowers fresh and green;
All sorts of pleasant dainty fruits
  At all times there are to be seen.

The lily white, the ruddy rose,
  The crimson and carnation flowers
Be watered there with honey dews
  And heavenly drops of golden showers.
Pomegranate (prince of fruit), the peach,
  The dainty date and pleasant fig,
The almond, muscatel, and grape,
  Exceeding good and wondrous big.

The lemon, orange medlar, quince,
  The apricot and Indian spice,
The cherry, warden plum and pear—
  More sorts than were in Paradise—
The fruit more eyesome, toothsome, fair
  Than that which grew on Adam's tree;
For whose delights assailed were
  And both suppressed Eve and he.

The swelling, odoriferous balm
  Most sweetly there doth sweat and drop;

The fruitful and victorious palm
  Lays out her lofty mountain top;
The river wine most pleasant flows,
  More pleasant than the honey comb,
Upon whose banks the sugar grows,
  Enclosed in reeds of cinnamon.

The walls of jasper stone be built,
  Most rich and fair that ever was;
The streets and houses paved and gilt
  With gold more clear than crystal glass.
Her gates in equal distance be
  And each a glistering marguerite;
Which comers-in far off may see—
  A gladsome and a glorious sight.

Her inward chambers of delight
  Be checked with pearl and precious stone;
The doors and posterns all be white,
  Of wrought and burnished ivory bone.
Her sun doth never eclipse nor cloud,
  Her moon doth never there wax wane;
The Lamb with light hath her endowed,
  Whose glory pen can ne'r explain.

The glorious saints there dwellers be,
  In number more than man can think,
So many in a company,
  As love in likeness doth them link.
The stars, in brightness, they do pass;
  In swiftness, arrows from a bow;
In strength, in firmness, steel and brass,
  In lightness, fire, in whiteness snow.

Their clothing is more soft than silk,
  With girdles girt of beaten gold;
They in their hands (more white than milk)
  Of palm triumphant, branches hold;
Their faces shining like the sun,
  Shoot out their gladsome glorious beams;
The field is fought, the battle won,
  Their heads be crowned with diadems.

Reward, as merit, different is,
  Distinct, their joy and happiness;
But each in joy of other's bliss,
  Doth as his own, the same possess;
So each in glory doth abound,
  And all in glory doth excel;
But whereas all to each redound,
  Who can the exceeding glory tell?

Triumphant martyrs, you may hear
  Recount their dangers, which do cease.
And noble citizens ever wear
  Their happy gowns of joy and peace.
There learned clerks, with sharpened wits,
  Their maker's wondrous works do tell.
The Judges, grave, on bench do sit
  To judge the tribes of Israel.

The glorious courtiers over there
  Attend on person of their King;
With angels, joined in a choir,
  Melodious hymns of praises sing.
The virgin chaste, in lily white,
  The martyrs clad in scarlet red.

The holy fathers who did write,
  Wear laurel garlands on their heads.

Each Confessor a golden crown,
  Adorned with pearl and precious stone,
Th'Apostles (peerless in renown)
  Like princes sit on regal throne;
Queen mother, virgin imminent—
  Than saints and angels more divine;
Like sun amidst the firmament,
  Above the planets all doth shine.

The King, that heavenly palace rules,
  Doth bear upon his golden shield
A cross in sign of triumph—gules,
  Erected in a verdant field.
His glory saith as doth behove,
  Him in his manhood for to take,
Whose Godhead earth and heaven above,
  And all that dwell therein did make.

Like friends all partners are in bliss,
  With Christ their Lord and master dear
Like spouses, they the Bridegroom kiss,
  Who feasteth them with heavenly cheer;
With tree of life and manna sweet,
  Which, tasted, doth such pleasure bring;
As none to judge thereof be meet
  But such as banquet with the King.

With cherubims their wings they move,
  And mount in contemplation high;
With seraphims they burn in love,
  The beams of glory be so nigh.

The Virgin's children dear they be,
  Her loving Son for to embrace;
And Jesus, his brethren, for to see,
  His heavenly Father's glorious face.

Oh sweet aspect, vision of peace,
  Happy regard and heavenly sight!
Oh endless joy, without surcease,
  Perpetual day, which hath no night!
Oh well and vale, fountain of life,
  Of spring of everlasting bliss;
Eternal sun, resplendent light,
  And eminent cause of all that is.

River of pleasure, sea of delight,
  Garden of glory, ever green!
Oh glorious glass and mirror bright,
  Wherein all truth is ever seen!
Oh princely palace, royal court,
  Monarchal seat, imperial throne;
Where King of Kings and Sovereign Lord
  Forever ruleth all alone—

Where all the glorious saints do see
  The secrets of the Deity—
The Godhead, and in persons three,
  The super-blessed Trinity;
The depth of wisdom most profound
  All puissant, high sublimity;
The breadth of love, without all bound,
  In endless long eternity.

The heavy Earth below by kind,
  Above ascends the mounting fire;

Be this the center of my mind,
  And lofty spear of her desire!
The chased deer do take the soil,
  The tired hart the thick and wood;
Be this the comfort of my toil,
  My refuge, hope and sovereign good.

The merchant cleaves the sea for gain,
  The soldier serves for his renown,
The tillman plows the ground for grain—
  Be this my joy and lasting crown!
The falconer seeks to see a flight,
  The hunter beats to see his game
Long then, my soul, to see that sight
  And labor to enjoy the same.

No hour without some one delight
  Which he endeavors to attain;
Seek thou, my soul, both day and night
  This one, which ever shall remain:
This one contains all pleasure true,
  All other pleasures are but vain;
Bid thou the rest, my soul, adieu,
  And seek alone this one to gain.

Go count the grass upon the ground,
  Or sands that be upon the shore;
And when you have the number found,
  The joys thereof be many more.
More thousand, thousand years they last
  And lodge within the happy mind;
And when so many years be past,
  Yet more and more be still behind.
Far more they be than we can ween,

They do our judgment much excel;
No ear hath heard or eye hath seen,
No pen can write, no tongue can tell.
An angel's tongue cannot recite
The endless joys of heavenly bliss,
Which being wholly infinite,
Beyond all speech and writing is.
We can imagine but a shade
It never entered into thought
What joy he is enjoyn'd that made
All joy and them that joy, of naught
My soul cannot the joys contain—
Let her, Lord, enter into them,
Forever with thee to remain
Within thy town Hierusalem.†

† **Note by Fr. O'Connell:** This poem has a special interest, as it appears in the British Museum Add MMS, 15, 225, fol, 39-42, without any author's name, and there seems to be some doubt as to its authorship. It has been ascribed by Fr. J. H. Pollen, S.J., Dr. Hyder Rollins, Dr. Augustus H. Jessop and other authorities to the Blessed Father Henry Walpole, S.J., on grounds which appear to be fairly convincing. There is reason to believe that it was written by Father Walpole during the period of his imprisonment in the Tower (March, 1594, to April, 1595) when he was seeking consolation for the death which he could not but foresee he was soon to suffer, by the contemplation of that celestial life which would be the reward of his martyrdom. "Hierusalem my happy home" has been ascribed to St. Augustine, though a somewhat similar poem appears to have been written by Bernard de Morlaix, a monk of Cluny, and St. Peter Damien's hymn, *Ad perennis vitae fontem mens sitivit arída*, "My thirsty soul desires her draught," with its undersong, "Jerusalem my joys divine," may well have inspired the Blessed Henry Walpole. In its English rendering there were many versions, especially during the sixteenth century, when the sufferings of the martyrs in prison and the anticipation of the terrible death which awaited them naturally turned their thoughts to the reward which their witness to the Faith would win for them. Blessed Henry Walpole's rendering of this poem is considerably longer and more detailed in its description of the delights of the Heavenly City than any of the other versions which have hitherto been published. The spelling, which is somewhat archaic in the British Museum MMS, has been modernized in the version given above, but otherwise the poem is printed as it appears in the British Museum MMS.

SAINT ROBERT SOUTHWELL, S.J.

(1561–FEBRUARY 21, 1595)

> Among them was Margaret, a maiden among a thousand, in whose frail sex shone a courage hard to parallel. Together with her friend, an Irishman named Roche, she suffered death for supplying a priest in prison with the rope whereby he escaped. She had been flogged and hung up by the wrists, the tips of her toes only touching the ground, so that she was now crippled and half-paralyzed; but the tortures had only served to strengthen this most shining martyr for her last struggle.[1]

SO WROTE ROBERT SOUTHWELL in a letter to the Superior General of the Jesuits, Claudio Aquaviva, in 1588. Southwell was recounting the flurry of executions that he witnessed in England following the disastrous voyage of the Spanish Armada and the consequent intensification of the religious persecutions. The woman he describes was Margaret Ward; she was hung on August 30, 1588, at Tyburn, along with a priest, Richard Leigh, and three other Catholic men.

Robert Southwell was clearly inspired by Margaret, who sang the *Te Deum* as she was carted to Tyburn and was blessed by Fr. Leigh as she bravely ascended the scaffold, but these were far from the only executions he witnessed. From 1586 to 1592, Southwell lived in England, ministering to the recusant Catholic population, secretly publishing works to comfort and strengthen them, and helping to find suitable hidden lodgings for the new priests who arrived from the continent. It was a dangerous mission for any priest to undertake, and Southwell spent most of his six years in London, even as the government gradually became more and more aware of his presence and influence, and increased its efforts to capture him. During these years, Southwell bore witness to many executions—some, like Margaret Ward's, drawing words of praise from Southwell, although it is unclear if he knew her personally. Other tortures and executions were inflicted upon people very close to Southwell, including laymen who sheltered him and his fellow priests, as well as young priests who had been his students at the English College in Rome just a few years before, and who now were martyred before their teacher. Southwell was moved by often conflicting passions—sorrow at the martyrs' suffering and loss, inspiration at their strong faith—and these contending sentiments have a pronounced influence upon his poetry and prose writings. After all, Christ's example (a theme to which Southwell returns repeatedly in his poetry) is the perfection of martyrdom, a sacrifice at once both terrible and wonderful.

Robert Southwell was born into a wealthy and well-connected family in 1561. His family was inclined towards the Catholic faith, though with varying consistency. His paternal grandfather, Richard Southwell, served the English government under Henry VIII, and was greatly enriched during the dissolution and pillaging of the monasteries beginning in 1536. He also wrote an appeal, however, in defense of at least one priory, and more famously, he refused to provide evidence against Thomas More

1. Christopher Devlin, *The Life of Robert Southwell, Poet and Martyr* (New York: Longmans, Green and Co., 1956), p. 175.

during his trial. In his later life, he was accused of being staunchly anti-Protestant. His son, Robert's father, also named Richard, was raised Catholic but wavered, such that when Robert returned to England after his education and ordination in Rome, he wrote *An Epistle Unto His Father*, a powerful letter urging his father to repent his attendance at the Church of England services and return to the Catholic faith. The letter was copied frequently and circulated widely throughout the 1580s, and was printed for wider distribution by fellow-Jesuit Henry Garnet's secret printing press. While the immediate influence of the letter upon Robert's father is unknown, his name appears on the government lists of recusants in 1588, and he was later imprisoned in the Fleet Prison. In a letter to Aquaviva in 1600, Fr. Garnet wrote, "Mr. Southwell, Robert's Father, had just died a Catholic."[2] It seems likely that Robert's mother was a firm Catholic, and that she played an important part in shaping his deep attachment to the Catholic Church in his youth.

In 1576, at the age of fifteen, Southwell left England for the English College at Douai (established by William Allen to educate Catholic Englishmen for the priesthood). After two years of study, he made his way to Rome with some fellow students, determined to join the Society of Jesus. Southwell's first application to the Jesuits was rejected, but on an impassioned and desperate appeal, he was accepted as a novice. He became acquainted with many people of interest during his studies in Rome, including some of the great Jesuits of the time, St. Robert Bellarmine and the scholastic philosopher Francisco Suárez. Furthermore, he knew St. Edmund Campion slightly and admired him greatly, and Campion's companion on the first English mission, Fr. Robert Persons, was Southwell's spiritual director and close friend. One other student novice whom Southwell met and lived with in Rome was Simon Hunt, who, prior to his becoming a Jesuit, had

2. Ibid., p. 203.

been the schoolmaster in Stratford-Upon-Avon, and had taught the young William Shakespeare his first courses in school.

Southwell took his first vows in 1580, and was ordained in 1584, at the tender age of twenty-three. Belying his youth, he had shown a remarkable intellectual talent and deep dedication to his studies. By the time of his ordination, he had already served as a tutor in the English College for two years, and was made the Prefect of Studies for the whole college. Indeed, when he performed his "Public Defense" at the completion of his studies in philosophy, one of his companions wrote, "His excellent talents and abundance of divine light enabled him to make such quick progress that—I say so in all moderation—he was without a rival in philosophy among his fellow-students of the Roman College, which is the most celebrated in the world."[3]

Despite his important place in shaping and educating the new English Jesuits, Southwell desired to follow in Campion's footsteps and return to England to minister to the beleaguered Catholics there. Campion had been caught in England in 1581 after barely more than a year of clandestine missionary service, and was hung, drawn, and quartered by the end of that year. In 1586, Southwell was granted his wish to return to England, and made the journey with his fellow Jesuit Henry Garnet. Southwell and Garnet were warmly welcomed and given immediate shelter by several great Catholic families in London, including at the house of Lord William Vaux of Harrowden, who had himself been repeatedly convicted and imprisoned for being a Catholic and harboring and aiding priests (including Edmund Campion). His son, Henry Vaux (see Appendix, pp. 211–16), was himself a poet and died from illness contracted while imprisoned for harboring priests.

Southwell also formed a connection with the reclusive Countess Anne Howard, the long-suffering wife of the imprisoned

3. Ibid., p. 46.

Philip Howard, Earl of Arundel and Surrey. Philip was himself a poet, and soon-to-be martyr for the Catholic faith, despite holding one of the most significant titles in the English peerage and having been one of Queen Elizabeth's noted courtiers before he repented and professed Catholicism. Anne Howard provided Southwell with secret lodgings and supported him financially; she even helped him establish a Catholic printing press so that he could print and circulate devotional tracts and theological polemics. In return for this support, he counselled and consoled both Anne and Philip as Philip remained in prison. Several letters between Southwell and Philip survive, and although the former served almost as a personal chaplain to Anne while he stayed in their house, and both were finally imprisoned in the Tower of London in 1595, it seems likely that these two poets, friends, and martyrs never met in person.

Southwell was inspired by the faith of the English Catholics he served, and by their willingness to sacrifice everything for the faith. To take one example, in late 1586 (just months after he arrived in England), the discovery of the Babington Plot provoked a great increase in anti-Catholic fervor and persecution. The conspirators involved in the Babington Plot planned to assassinate Queen Elizabeth and place the Catholic Mary Queen of Scots on the throne. Though Southwell and his companions repeatedly insisted that their mission had no political ends, and that their only reason for returning to England was to minister to souls, Southwell was deeply worried that even the Catholics would regard him and his companions with suspicion, as disloyal traitors to the English people. His joy at finding the opposite to be the case is captured in a letter he wrote shortly after he returned to London:

> And yet the faith is still alive! The Church exults! The families are not falling away. The work of God is being pressed forward—often enough by delicate women who have taken on the courage of men. For as

> the sufferings of Christ abound in us, so also through Christ abounds our consolation. Only priests are lacking. It is clear and certain that, whatever storms are raging, the Bark of Peter is moving forward, and moving steadily, and very many are seeking access to her. Let them come, then, those who are to come, so that the fruits of our toil may be greater.[4]

One of Robert Southwell's most popular prose works, *Mary Magdalene's Funeral Tears* (1591), which was begun in Rome but completed and printed in England, was composed as a comfort and guide to English Catholics who felt abandoned or isolated. It is an extended meditation on the nature of Mary Magdalen's sorrows in the hours following Christ's crucifixion and death, and contains profound reflections on her overwhelming feelings of loss and grief. It is a deeply imaginative and passionate work, and presents in prose some of the common motifs and strains found in his verse as well. Published by a commercial printer, the work became popular among Catholics and Protestants alike and was frequently reprinted and excerpted. Likewise, his *A Shorte Rule of Good Life*, dedicated to Anne Howard, Countess of Arundel, became a popular work, giving practical steps for living a life of devotion and increasing holiness. Versions of this, edited for Protestant use, were published several times.

After six years of hiding in London, administering sacraments, circulating works to inspire Catholics and defend the Catholic faith, and witnessing many martyrdoms, Southwell was finally captured. On June 25, 1592, he spent the night at the house of the Bellamy family in Uxenden, en route to meet his companion Fr. Garnet. The Bellamy family were quite close with the Jesuits and well-known as loyal Catholics who frequently harbored priests. Yet, the eldest daughter of the family, Anne, had been

4. Ibid., p. 140.

imprisoned, tortured, and impregnated by Richard Topcliffe, Queen Elizabeth's notoriously vicious hunter of priests. Topcliffe was a brutal, cunning man, so devoted to torture that he had a rack installed at his home. He had broken Anne Bellamy, who betrayed twenty-six Catholics, including her parents, and Robert Southwell. When Southwell stayed at the Bellamy house on the night of June 25, Topcliffe and his agents broke upon them, capturing Southwell. He was immediately taken to Topcliffe's house and tortured, but confessed nothing, and on July 28 he was committed to the Tower of London.

Although the English government had been most energetic in its hunt for Southwell, it now surprisingly left him to languish in prison for more than two years before he was brought to trial. He readily admitted that he was a Jesuit priest, but continually insisted upon his loyalty to Elizabeth as rightful queen of England, his lack of political aims, and his sole mission in England as one of spiritual ministry to Catholics. Ten different times Southwell was tortured until he was incapable of response, and between these brutal sessions, he was locked in solitary confinement, too enfeebled to even raise himself from the floor, or clean or relieve himself. Finally brought to trial on February 20, 1595, he was physically broken and extremely weak, but his hardiness under torture, and his intellectual readiness in defense of himself so infuriated his torturer that Topcliffe had to be restrained several times from attacking him while the court was in session. By several accounts, it was quite clear who had actually gained the upper hand between the torturer and the tortured. The only evidence given against him was by Anne Bellamy, who merely testified that he had said it was permissible to conceal priests from government agents. Nevertheless, he was convicted of treason, and sentenced to be hung, drawn, and quartered.

On the day following his trial, February 21, 1595, Southwell was taken to Tyburn, where many English Catholics died, including Edmund Campion and Margaret Ward (whom Southwell had praised so highly). Contemporary accounts record his peaceful resignation and his final prayer upon the scaffold, which was offered for the conversion and salvation of Queen Elizabeth, for England, and for his own soul's perseverance to the end. His final words, standing on a cart with the noose about his neck, were, "*In manus tuas, Domine*," but when the cart was jerked away, the execution did not follow the prescribed process. Normally, the person being hung, drawn, and quartered would be cut down from the scaffold while still conscious, to have his stomach cut open and his organs ripped out in front of him. But the crowd watching Southwell's execution (including some powerful Protestant nobles) interfered when the Sheriff came forward to cut the rope. The Sheriff drew his sword and called them traitors, but the crowd would not allow him near to Southwell, and the Protestant Lord Mountjoy retorted, "I cannot answer for his religion, but I wish to God that my soul may be with his."[5] Then the executioner himself grabbed Southwell's ankles and pulled down, mercifully hastening Southwell's death by hanging, and sparing him consciousness during the evisceration. When his corpse was beheaded and the head lifted before the crowd, none chanted the customary "Traitor"; instead, silence filled Tyburn.

Robert Southwell's poetry was first gathered probably by his companion Fr. Garnet, following his arrest. The poems were compiled and first printed in 1595, and were frequently reprinted in the following years. In these early editions, the poems that struck more explicitly Catholic notes were often omitted, with the consequence that Southwell quickly gained a wide readership, as Protestant and Catholic alike found much to admire. His poetry is clearly influenced by the imaginative, contemplative depths reached through the Ignatian meditative method of Jesuits. In keeping with this tradition, a simple scene or image may govern the poem, but it will be developed often in quite complex

5. Ibid., p. 324.

ways. Southwell embraces paradox and passion, intellectual complexity and emotional responsiveness. The poems regularly exhibit a quick and sophisticated intellectual thrust that is paired with a devout sensibility that surpasses anything strictly logical or dialectical. His theme is always, unapologetically spiritual, as he continually places temporal, earthly existence in the context of mankind's transcendent and final end.

Sources and Further Reading

Brown, Nancy Pollard. "Robert Southwell [St. Robert Southwell] (1561–1595)." In *Oxford Dictionary of National Biography.* New York: Oxford University Press, 2004.

Devlin, Christopher. *The Life of Robert Southwell, Poet and Martyr.* New York: Longmans, Green and Co., 1956.

Southwell, Robert. *Collected Poems.* Edited by Peter Davidson and Anne Sweeney. Manchester: Carcanet Press Limited, 2007.

Southwell, Robert. *Two Letters and Short Rules of a Good Life.* Edited by Nancy Pollard Brown. Folger Shakespeare Library. Charlottesville: University Press of Virginia, 1973.

Undset, Sigrid. "Robert Southwell, S.J.: Priest, Poet, Martyr." In *Stages on the Road.* Translated by Arthur G. Chater, pp. 105–138. Notre Dame, IN: Christian Classics, 2012.

The Poetry of Saint Robert Southwell, S.J

‡ ‡ ‡

The Burning Babe

As I in hoary winter's night stood shivering in the snow,
Surprised I was with sudden heat which made my heart
to glow;
And lifting up a fearful eye to view what fire was near,
A pretty Babe all burning bright did in the air appear;
Who, scorched with excessive heat, such floods of tears
did shed,
As though his floods should quench his flames which with
his tears were fed.
"Alas!" quoth he, "but newly-born, in fiery heats I fry,
Yet none approach to warm their hearts or feel my fire but I.
My faultless breast the furnace is, the fuel wounding thorns;
Love is the fire, and sighs the smoke, the ashes shame
and scorns;
The fuel Justice layeth on, and Mercy blows the coals;
The metal in this furnace wrought are men's defiled souls:
For which, as now on fire I am to work them to their good;
So will I melt into a bath to wash them in my blood."
With this he vanished out of sight and swiftly shrunk away,
And straight I called unto mind that it was Christmas day.

New Heaven, New War

Come to your heaven, you heavenly choirs!
Earth hath the heaven of your desires;
Remove your dwelling to your God,
A stall is now his best abode;
Since men their homage do deny,
Come, angels, all their fault supply.

His chilling cold doth heat require,
Come, seraphims, in lieu of fire;
This little ark no cover hath,
Let cherubs' wings his body swathe;
Come, Raphael, this Babe must eat,
Provide our little Toby meat.

Let Gabriel be now his groom,
That first took up his earthly room;
Let Michael stand in his defense,
Whom love hath linked to feeble sense;
Let graces rock when he doth cry,
And angels sing his lullaby.

The same you saw in heavenly seat,
Is he that now sucks Mary's teat;
Agnize[6] your King a mortal wight,
His borrowed weed lets not your sight,
Come, kiss the manger where he lies,
That is your bliss above the skies.

This little Babe, so few days old,
Is come to rifle Satan's fold;

6. "Agnize," meaning *acknowledge*.

All hell doth at his presence quake,
Though he himself for cold do shake;
For in his weak unarmed wise
The gates of hell he will surprise.

With tears he fights and wins the field,
His naked breast stands for a shield;
His battering shot are babish cries,
His arrows looks of weeping eyes,
His martial ensigns cold and need,
And feeble flesh his warrior's steed.

His camp is pitched in a stall,
His bulwark but a broken wall;
The crib his trench, hay-stalks his stakes,
Of shepherds he his muster makes;
And thus, as sure his foe to wound,
The angels' trumps alarum sound.

My soul, with Christ join thou in fight;
Stick to the tents that he hath pight[7]:
Within his crib is surest ward,
This little Babe will be thy guard;
If thou wilt foil thy foes with joy,
Then flit not from this heavenly boy.

7. "Pight," meaning *pitched*.

New Prince, New Pomp

Behold, a silly[8] tender Babe
In freezing winter night
In homely manger trembling lies,
Alas, a piteous sight!

The inns are full; no man will yield
This little pilgrim bed,
But forced he is with silly beasts
In crib to shroud his head.

Despise him not for lying there,
First, what he is inquire;
An orient pearl is often found
In depth of dirty mire.

Weigh not his crib, his wooden dish,
Nor beasts that by him feed;
Weigh not his mother's poor attire,
Nor Joseph's simple weed.

This stable is a Prince's court,
This crib his chair of state;
The beasts are parcel of his pomp,
The wooden dish his plate.

The persons in that poor attire,
His royal liveries wear;
The Prince himself is come from heaven;
This pomp is prized there.

8. "Silly," meaning *simple* or *innocent*.

With joy approach, Oh Christian wight,
  Do homage to thy King;
And highly praise his humble pomp,
  Which he from heaven doth bring.

Our Lady's Salutation

Spell *Eva* back and *Ave* shall you find,
  The first began, the last reversed our harms;
An angel's witching words did Eva blind,
  An angel's Ave disenchants the charms;
Death first by woman's weakness entered in,
In woman's virtue life doth now begin.

Oh virgin blessed! The heavens to thee incline,
  In thee their joy and sovereign they recognize;
Too mean their glory is to match with thine,
  Whose chaste receipt God more than heaven did prize.
Hail, fairest heaven, that heaven and earth doth bliss,
Where virtues stares, God son of justice is!

With haughty mind to Godhead man aspired,
  And was by pride from place of pleasure chased;.
With loving mind our manhead God desired,
  And us by love in greater pleasure placed:
Man laboring to ascend procured our fall,
God yielding to descent cut off our thrall.

The Nativity of Christ

Behold the father is his daughter's son,
  The bird that built the nest is hatched therein,
The old of years an hour hath not out run,
  Eternal life to live doth now begin,
The word is dumb, the mirth of heaven doth weep,
Might feeble is, and force doth faintly creep.

Oh dying souls, I behold your living spring!
  Oh dazzled eyes! behold your Sun of Grace!
Dull ears, attend what word this Word doth bring!
  Up, heavy hearts, with joy your joy embrace!
From death, from dark, from deafness, from despair,
This Life, this Light, this Word, this Joy repairs.

Gift better than himself God doth not know,
  Gift better than his God no man can see;
This gift doth here the giver given bestow,
  Gift to this gift let each receiver be:
God is my gift, himself he freely gave me
God's gift am I, and none but God shall have me.

Man altered was by sin from man to beast;
  Beast's food is hay, hay is all mortal flesh;
Now God is flesh, and lies in manger pressed,
  As hay the brutest sinner to refresh:
Oh happy field wherein this fodder grew,
Whose taste doth us from beasts to men renew!

The Epiphany

To blaze the rising of this glorious sun,
  A glittering star appeared in the East,
Whose sight to pilgrim-toils three sages won,
  To seek the light they long had in request;
And by this star to nobler star they pace,
Whose arms did their desired sun embrace.

Stall was the sky wherein these planets shine,
  And want the cloud that did eclipse their rays;
Yet through this cloud their light did passage find,
  And pierced these sages' hearts by secret ways,
Which made them know the Ruler of the skies,
By infant tongue and looks of babyish eyes.

Heaven at her light, Earth blusheth at her pride,
  And of their pomp these peers ashamed be;
Their crowns, their robes, their train they set aside,
  When God's poor cottage, clothes and crew they see;
All glorious things their glory now despise,
Since God contempt doth more than glory prize.

Three gifts they bring, three gifts they bear away;
  For incense, myrrh and gold; faith, hope and love;
And with their gifts the givers' hearts do stay,
  Their mind from Christ no parting can remove;
His humble state, his stall, his poor retinue
They fancy more than all their rich revenue.

Christ's Childhood

Till twelve years' age, how Christ his childhood spent
  All earthly pens unworthy were to write;
Such acts to mortal eyes he did present,
  Whose worth not men but angels must recite:
No nature's blots, no childish faults defiled,
Where grace was guide, and God did play the child.

In springing locks lay couchèd hoary wit,
  In semblance young, a grave and ancient port;
In lowly looks high majesty did sit,
  In tender tongue, sound sense of sagest sort:
Nature imparted all that she could teach,
And God supplied where Nature could not reach.

His mirth, of modest mean a mirror was,
  His sadness tempered with a mild aspect;
His eye, to try each action was a glass,
  Whose looks did good approve and bad correct;
His Nature's gifts, his grace, his word and deed,
Well show'd that all did from a God proceed.

A Child My Choice

Let folly praise what fancy loves, I praise and love that Child
Whose heart no thought, whose tongue no word, whose hand
no deed defiled.

I praise him most, I love him best, all praise and love is his;
While him I love, in him I live, and cannot live amiss.

Love's sweetest mark, laud's highest theme, man's most
desired light:
To love him life, to leave him death, to live in him delight.

He mine by gift, I his by debt, thus each to other due,
First friend he was, best friend he is, all times will try him true.

Though young, yet wise, though small, yet strong; though man,
yet God he is;
As wise he knows, as strong he can, as God he loves to bliss.

His knowledge rules, his strength defends, his love doth
cherish all;
His birth our joy, his life our light, his death our end of thrall.

Alas, he weeps, he sighs, he pants, yet do his angels sing;
Out of his tears, his sighs, and throbs, doth bud a joyful spring.

Almighty babe, whose tender arms can force all foes to fly,
Correct my faults, protect my life, direct me when I die.

Sin's Heavy Load

Oh Lord! my sin doth overcharge thy breast.
  The poise thereof doth force thy knees to bow;
Yea, flat thou fallest with my faults oppressed,
  And bloody sweat run trickling from thy brow:
But had they not to earth thus pressed thee,
Much more they would in hell have pestered me.

This globe of earth doth thy one finger prop,
  The world thou dost within thy hand embrace;
Yet all this weight, of sweat drew not a drop,
  Nor made thee bow, much less fall on thy face;
But now thou hast a load so heavy found
That makes thee bow, yea flat fall to the ground.

Oh Sin! how huge and heavy is thy weight,
  Thou weighest more than all the world beside;
Of which when Christ had taken in his freight,
  The weight thereof his flesh could not abide.
Alas! if God himself sink under sin,
What will become of man that dies therein?

First flat thou fallest where earth did thee receive,
  In closet pure of Mary's virgin breast;
And now thou fallest, of earth to take thy leave,
  Thou kissed it as cause of thy unrest:
Oh loving Lord! that so dost love thy foe
As thus to kiss the ground where he doth go!

Thou, minded in thy heaven our earth to wear,
  Dost prostrate now thy heaven our earth to bliss;
As God to earth thou often wert severe,
  As man thou sealst a peace with bleeding kiss:

For as of soul thou common father art,
So is she mother of man's other part.

She shortly was to drink thy dearest blood,
  And yield thy soul away to Satan's cave;
She shortly was thy corpse in tomb to shroud,
  And with them all thy Deity to have;
Now then in one thou jointly yieldest all,
That severally to earth should shortly fall.

Oh prostrate Christ! erect my crooked mind;
  Lord! let thy fall my flight from earth obtain:
Or if I still in Earth must needs be shrin'd,
  Then, Lord! on Earth come fall yet once again;
And either yield with me in earth to lie,
Or else with thee to take me to the sky.

The Virgin Mary to Christ on the Cross

What mist hath dimmed that glorious face?
What seas of grief my sun doth toss?
The golden rays of heavenly grace lie now eclipsed on the cross.

Jesus! my Love, my Son, my God, behold thy mother washed
in tears;
Thy bloody wounds be made a rod to chasten these my
latter years.

You cruel Jews, come work your ire, upon this worthless flesh
of mine:
And kindle not eternal fire, by wounding him which is divine.

Thou messenger that didst impart his first descent into
my womb,
Come help me now to cleave my heart, that there I may
my Son entomb.

Ye angels all, that present were, to show his birth with harmony;
Why are you not now ready here, to make a mourning
symphony?

The cause I know, you wail alone and shed your tears
in secrecy,
Lest I should moved be to moan, by force of heavenly company.

But wail my soul, thy comfort dies, my woeful womb lament
thy fruit;
My heart, give tears unto my eyes, let sorrow string my
heavy lute.

Mary Magdalen's Complaint At Christ's Death

Since my life from life is parted
  Death come take thy portion;
Who survives when life is murdered,
  Lives by mere extortion;
All that live, and not in God,
Couch their life in death's abode.

Simple stars must needs leave shining
  When the sun is shadowed,
Borrowed streams refrain their running
  When head springs are hindered;
One that lives by other's breath,
Dieth also by his death.

Oh true life! Since thou hast left me,
  Mortal life is tedious
Death it is to live without thee,
  Death of all most odious:
Turn again or take me to thee,
Let me die or live thou in me!

Where the truth once was and is not,
  Shadows are but vanity,
Showing want, that help they cannot,
  Signs, not salves, of misery.
Painted meat no hunger feeds,
Dying life each death exceeds.

With my love my life was nestled
  In the sum of happiness:

From my love my life is wrested
  To a world of heaviness:
Oh let love my life remove,
Since I live not where I love!

Oh my soul! what did unloose thee
  From thy sweet captivity,
God, not I, did still possess thee,
  His, not mine, thy liberty:
Oh too happy thrall thou wert,
When thy prison was his heart.

Spiteful spear that brak'st this prison,
  Seat of all felicity,
Working thus with double treason
  Love's and life's delivery:
Though my life thou dravest away,
In spite of thee my love shall stay.

Man to the Wound in Christ's Side

Oh pleasant port! Oh place of rest!
  Oh royal rift! Oh worthy wound!
Come harbor me, a weary guest,
  That in the world no ease have found!

I lie lamenting at thy gate,
  Yet dare I not adventure in:
I bear with me a troublous mate,
  And cumbered am with heap of sin.

Discharge me of this heavy load,
  That easier passage I may find,
Within this bower to make abode,
  And in this glorious tomb be shrin'd.

Here must I live, here must I die,
  Here would I utter all my grief;
Here would I all those pains descry,
  Which here did meet for my relief.

Here would I view that bloody sore,[9]
  Which dint of spiteful spear did breed,
The bloody wounds laid there in store
  Would force a stony heart to bleed.

Here is the spring of trickling tears,
  The mirror of all mourning wights,

9. **Editor's Note:** These final three stanzas were omitted from the original *Lyra Martyrum*. The source text that has been modernized here is in Robert Southwell, S.J. *Collected Poems*, eds. Peter Davidson and Anne Sweeney (Manchester: Carcanet Press, 2007), p. 62.

With doleful tunes, for dumpish cares
  And solemn shows for sorrowed sights.

Oh happy soul that flies so high,
  As to attain this sacred cave:
Lord send me wings that I may fly,
  And in this harbor quiet have.

Life Is but Loss

By force I live, in will I wish to die,
In plaint I pass the length of lingering days;
Free would my soul from mortal body fly,
And tread the track of death's desired ways:
Life is but loss where death is deemed gain,
And loathed pleasures breed displeasing pain.

Who would not die to kill all murdering griefs?
Or who would live in never dying fears?
Who would not wish his treasure safe from thieves,
And quit his heart from pangs, his eyes from tears?
Death parteth but two ever-fighting foes,
Whose civil strife doth work our endless woes.

Life is a wandering course to doubtful rest,
As oft a cursed rise to damning leap,
As happy race to win a heavenly crest;
None being sure what final fruit to reap:
And who can like in such a life to dwell,
Whose ways are strait to heaven, but wide to hell?

Come, cruel death, why lingerest thou so long?
What doth withold thy dint from fatal stroke?
Now pressed I am, alas! thou dost me wrong,
To let me live, more anger to provoke:
Thy right is had when thou hast stopped my breath,
Why shouldst thou stay to work my double death?

If Saul's attempt in falling on his blade[10]

10. **Editor's Note:** This stanza was omitted from the original *Lyra Martyrum*. The source text that has been modernized here is in Southwell, *Collected Poems*, p. 45.

As lawful were as breath to put *in ure*,[11]
If Sampson's leave, a common law were made,
Of Abel's lot if all that would were sure,
Then cruel death thou should'st the tyrant play,
With none but such as wished for delay.

Where life is lov'd, thou ready art to kill,
And to abridge with sudden pangs their joy;
Where life is loathed thou wilt not work their will,
But dost adjourn their death to their annoy.
To some thou art a fierce unbidden guest,
But those that crave thy help thou helpest least.

Avaunt, Oh viper! I thy spite defy:
There is a God that overrules thy force,
Who can thy weapons to his will apply,
And shorten or prolong our brittle course.
I on his mercy, not thy might, rely;
To him I live, for him I hope to die.

11. "In ure," meaning *into use* or *into practice.*

I Die Alive

Oh life! what stays thee from a quick decease?
  Oh death! what draws thee from a present, pray?
My feast is done, my soul would be at ease,
  My grace is said; Oh death! Come take away.

I live, but such a life as ever dies;
  I die, but such a death as never ends;
My death to end my dying life denies,
  And life my living death no whit amends.

Thus still I die, yet still I do revive;
  My living death by dying life is fed;
Grace more than nature keeps my heart alive,
  Whose idle hopes and vain desires are dead.

Not where I breath, but where I love, I live;
  Not where I love, but where I am, I die;
The life I wish, must future glory give,
  The deaths I feel in present dangers lie.

Life's Death, Love's Life

Who lives in love, loves least to live,
  And long delays doth rue.
If him he love, by whom he lives,
  To whom all love is due;

Who for our love did choose to live,
  And was content to die;
Who loved our love more than his life,
  And love with life did buy;

Let us in life, yea with our life,
  Requite his living love.
For best we live when least we live,
  If love our life remove.

When love is hot, life hateful is,
  Their grounds do not agree;
Love where it loves, life where it lives,
  Desireth most to be.

And since love is not where it lives,
  Nor liveth where it loves,
Love hateth life that holds it back,
  And death it best approves.

For seldom is he won in life
  Whom love doth most desire;
If won by love, yet not enjoyed,
  Till mortal life expire.

Life out of earth hath no abode,
  In earth love hath no place;

Love settled hath her joys in heaven,
  In Earth life all her grace.

Mourn, therefore, no true lover's death,
  Life only him annoys;
And when he taketh leave of life,
  Then love begins his joys.

At Home in Heaven

Fair soul! how long shall veils thy graces shroud?
  How long shall this exile withhold thy right?
When with thy sun disperse this mortal cloud,
  And give thy glories scope to blaze their light?
Oh that a star, more fit for angel's eyes,
  Should pine in earth, not shine above the skies!

Thy ghostly beauty offered force to God;
  It chained him in the links of tender love;
It won his will with man to make abode;
  It stayed his sword, and did his wrath remove:
It made the rigor of his justice yield,
  And crowned Mercy empress of the field.

This lulled our heavenly Sampson fast asleep,
  And laid him in our feeble nature's lap;
This made him under mortal load to creep,
  And in our flesh his Godhead to enwrap;
This made him sojourn with us in exile,
  And not disdain our titles in his style.

This brought him from the ranks of heavenly choirs
  Into this vale of tears and cursed soil;
From flowers of grace into a world of briars,
  From life to death, from bliss to baleful toil.
This made him wander in our pilgrim-weed,
  And taste our torments to relieve our need.

Oh soul! do not thy noble thoughts abase,
  To loose thy loves in any mortal wight,
Content thy eye at home with native grace,
  Since God himself is ravished with thy sight;

If on thy beauty God enamored be,
  Base be thy love of any less than he.

Give not assent to muddy minded skill,
  That deems the feature of a pleasing face
To be the sweetest bait to lure the will;
  Not valuing right the worth of ghostly grace;
Let God's and angels' censure win belief,
  That of all beauties judge our souls the chief.

Queen Hester was of rare and peerless hue,
  And Judith once for beauty bore the vaunt;
But he that could our souls' endowments view
  Would soon to souls the crown of beauty grant.
Oh soul! out of thyself seek God alone:
  Grace more than thine, but God's, the world hath none.

Look Home

Retired thoughts enjoy their own delights,
As beauty doth in self-beholding eye;
Man's mind a mirror is of heavenly sights,
A brief wherein all marvels summoned lie,
Of fairest forms and sweetest shapes the store,
Most graceful all, yet thought may grace them more.

The mind a creature is, yet can create,
To Nature's patterns adding higher skill;
Of finest works wit better could the state
If force of wit had equal power of will:
Devise of man in working hath no end;
What thought can think another thought can mend.

Man's soul of endless beauty's image is,
Drawn by the work of endless skill and might;
This skillful might gave many sparks of bliss,
And to discern this bliss a native light;
To frame God's image as his worth required,
His might, his skill, his word and will conspir'd.

All that he had his image should present,
All that it should present he could afford,
To that he could afford his will was bent,
His will was followed with performing word;
Let this suffice, by this conceive the rest,
He should, he could, he would, he did the best.

Seek Flowers in Heaven

Soar up, my soul, unto thy rest,
Cast off this loathsome load,
Long is the date of thy exile,
Too long thy strait abode.

Graze not on worldly withered weed,
It fitteth not thy taste;
The flowers of everlasting spring
Do grow for thy repast.

Their leaves are stained in beauty's dye,
And biased with their beams,
Their stalks enameled with delight,
And limed with glorious gleams.

Life-giving juice of living love
Their sugared veins doth fill,
And watered with eternal showers
They nectared drops distill.

These flowers do spring from fertile soil,
Though from unmanur'd field,[12]
Most glittering gold in lieu of glebe,
These fragrant flowers doth yield.

Whose sovereign scent surpassing sense
So ravisheth the mind,
That worldly weeds needs must he loathe
That can these flowers find.

12. "Glebe," meaning a *clod of earth* or a *plot of land.*

Saint Thomas Aquinas' Hymn for Corpus Christi Day

LAUDA SION SALVATOREM

Praise, Oh Sion! praise thy Savior,
Praise thy captain and thy pastor,
With hymns and solemn harmony.
What pour affords, perform in deed;
His worth all praises far exceed,
No praise can reach his dignity.

A special theme of praise is read,
A living and life-giving bread,
Is on this day exhibited;
Which in the supper of our Lord,
To twelve disciples at his board
None doubts but was delivered.

Let our praise be loud and free,
Full of joy and decent glee,
With minds and voices' melody;
For now solemnize we that day,
Which doth with joy to us display
The prime use of this mystery.

At this board of our new ruler,
Of new law, new paschal order
The ancient rite abolisheth,
Old decrees by new annulled,
Shadows are in truths fulfilled,
Day former darkness finisheth.

That at supper Christ performed,
To be done he straightly charged
  For his eternal memory.
Guided by his sacred orders,
Bread and wine upon our altars
  To saving Host we sanctify.

Christians are by faith assured
That to flesh the bread is changed,
  The wine to blood most precious:
That no wit nor sense conceiveth,
Firm and grounded faith believeth,
  In strange effects not curious.

Under kinds two in appearance,
Two in show, but one in substance,
  Lie things beyond comparison;
Flesh is meat, blood drink most heavenly,
Yet is Christ in each kind wholly,
  Most free from all division.

None that eateth him doth chew him,
None that takes him doth divide him,
  Received, he whole persevereth.
Be there one or thousands houseled,[13]
One as much as all received,
  He by no eating perisheth.

Both the good and bad receive him,
But effects are diverse in them,
  True life or due destruction.
Life to the good, death to the wicked,

13. "Houseled," meaning *given the Eucharist*.

Mark how both alike received
  With far unlike conclusion.

When the priest the Host divideth,
Know that in each part abideth
  All that the whole Host covered.
Form of bread, not Christ is broken,
Not of Christ but of his token,
  Is state or stature altered.

Angels' bread made pilgrims' feeding,
Truly bread for children's eating,
  To dog not to be offered.
Signed by Isaac on the altar,
By the Lamb and paschal supper,
  And in the manna figured.

Jesu, food and feeder of us,
Here with mercy, feed and friend us,
  Then grant in heaven felicity!
Lord of all, whom here thou feedest,
Fellows, heirs, guests with thy dearest,
  Make us in heavenly company. Amen.

Of the Blessed Sacrament of the Altar

In paschal feast, the end of ancient rite,
An entrance was to never-ending grace;
Types to the truth, dim glimpses to the light;
Performing deed presaging signs did chase:
Christ's final meal was fountain of our good,
For mortal meat he gave immortal food.

That which he gave, he was: Oh peerless gift!
Both God and man he was, and both he gave.
He in his hands himself did truly lift,
Far off they see whom in themselves they have;
Twelve did he feed, twelve did their feeder eat,
He made, he dressed, he gave, he was their meat.

They saw, they heard, they felt him sitting near,
Unseen, unfelt, unheard, they him received;
No diverse thing, though diverse it appear;
Though senses fail, yet faith is not deceived;
And if the wonder of the work be new,
Believe the work because his word is true.

Here truth believe, belief inviteth love,
So sweet a truth Love never yet enjoyed;
What thought can think, what will doth best approve,
Is here obtained where no desire is void:
The grace, the joy, the treasure here is such,
No wit can wish, nor will embrace so much.

Self-love here cannot crave more than it finds;
Ambition to no higher worth aspire;
The eagrest famine of most hungry minds
May fill, yea far exceed their own desire:

In sum here is all in a sum expressed
Of much the most, of every good the best.

To ravish eyes here heavenly beauties are;
  To win the ear sweet music's sweetest sound;
To lure the taste the angels' heavenly fare;
  To sooth the scent divine perfumes abound;
To please the touch, he in our hearts doth bed,
Whose touch doth cure the deaf, the dumb, the dead.

Here to delight the wit true wisdom is,
  To woo the will—of every good the choice;
For memory, a mirror showing bliss;
  Here's all that can both sense and soul rejoice;
And if to all, all this it do not bring,
The fault is in the men, not in the thing.

Though blind men see no light, the sun doth shine;
  Sweet cakes are sweet, though fevered tastes deny it;
Pearls precious are, though trodden on by swine;
  Each truth is true, though all men do not try it;
The best still to the bad doth work the worst;
Things bred to bliss do make them more accursed.

The angels' eyes, whom veils cannot deceive,
  Might best disclose that best they do discern;
Men must with sound and silent faith receive
  More than they can by sense or reason learn;
God's pour our proofs, his works our wit exceed,
The Doers' might is reason of his deed.

A body is endued with ghostly rights;
  And Nature's work from Nature's law is free;
In heavenly sun lie hid eternal lights,

  Lights clear and near, yet them no eye can see
Dead forms a never-dying life do shroud;
A boundless sea lies in a little cloud.

The God of hosts in slender host doth dwell,
  Yea, God and man with all to either dew,
That God that rules the heavens and rifled hell,
  That man whose death did us to life renew:
That God and man that is the angels' bliss,
In form of bread and wine our nurture is.

Whole may his body be in smallest bread,
  Whole in the whole, yea whole in every crumb;
With which be one or be ten thousand fed,
  All to each one, to all but one doth come;
And though each one as much as all receive,
Not one too much, nor all too little have.

One soul in man is all in every part;
  One face at once in many mirrors shines;
One fearful noise doth make a thousand start;
  One eye at once of countless things defines;
If proofs of one in many, Nature frame,
God may in stranger sort perform the same.

God present is at once in every place,
  Yet God in every place is ever one;
So may there be by gifts of ghostly grace,
  One man in many rooms, yet filling none;
Since angels may effects of bodies show,
Gods' angels' gifts on bodies may bestow.

What God as author made, he alter may;
  No change so hard as making all of naught;

If Adam framèd were of slimy clay,
  Bread may to Christ's most sacred flesh be wrought:
He may do this that made with mighty hand
Of water wine, a snake of Moses' wand.

To the Christian Reader

If Virtue be thy guide,
True comfort is thy path,
And thou secure from erring steps,
That lead to vengeance wrath.

Not widest open door,
Nor spacious ways she goes;
To straight and narrow gate and way,
She calls, she leads, she shows.

She calls, the fewest come:
She leads, the humble spirited;
She shows them rest at race's end,
Soul's rest to heaven invited.

'Tis she that offers most;
'Tis she that most refuse;
'Tis she prevents the broad-way plagues,
Which most do willful choose.

Do choose the wide, the broad,
The left-hand way and gate:
These Vice applauds, these Virtue loathes
And teacheth hers to hate.

Her ways are pleasant ways,
Upon the right-hand side;
And heavenly-happy is that soul
Takes Virtue for her guide.

A Preparative to Prayer

When thou dost talk with God, by prayer I mean,
  Lift up pure hands, lay down all lust's desires:
Fix thoughts on heaven, present a conscience clean:
  Such holy balm, to mercy's throne aspires.
Confess faults' guilt, crave pardon for thy sin;
Tread holy paths, call grace to guide therein.

It is the spirit with reverence must obey
  Our maker's will, to practice what he taught;
Make not the flesh thy counsel when thou pray:
  'Tis enemy to every virtuous thought:
It is the foe we daily feed and clothe:
It is the prison that the soul doth loath.

Even as Elias, mounting to the sky,
  Did cast his mantle to the Earth behind:
So, when the heart presents the prayer on high,
  Exclude the world from traffic with the mind.
Lips near to God, and ranging heart within,
Is but vain babbling and converts to sin.

Like Abraham, ascending up the hill,
  To sacrifice; his servants left below,
That he might act the great commander's will,
  Without impeach to his obedient blow;
Even so the soul, remote from earthy things;
Should mount salvation's shelter, mercy's wings.

The Effects of Prayer

The sun by prayer did cease his course, and stayed;
The hungry lions fawned upon their prey;
A walled passage through the sea it made;
From furious fire it banished heat away;
It shut the heavens three years from giving rain,
It opened heavens, and clouds poured down again.

Ensamples of Our Savior

Our Savior (pattern of true holiness),
Continual prayed, us by ensample teaching,
When he was baptized in the wilderness,
In working miracles and in his preaching;
Upon the mount, in garden-groves of death,
At his Last Supper, at his parting breath.

Oh! fortress of the faithful, sure defense,
In which doth Christians' cognizance consist;
Their victory, their triumph comes from thence,
So forcible, hell-gates cannot resist:
A thing whereby both angels, clouds, and stars,
At man's request fight God's revengeful wars.

Nothing more grateful in the highest eyes,
Nothing more firm in danger to protect us,
Nothing more forcible to pierce the skies,
And not depart till Mercy do respect us:
And, as the soul life to the body gives,
So prayer revives the soul, by prayer it lives.

Content and Rich

I dwell in Grace's court,
  Enriched with Virtue's rights;
Faith guides my wit, Love leads my will,
  Hope all my mind delights.

In lowly vales I mount
  To pleasure's highest pitch;
My silly[14] shroud true honor brings;
  My poor estate is rich.

My conscience is my crown,
  Contented thoughts my rest;
My heart is happy in itself;
  My bliss is in my breast.

Enough, I reckon wealth;
  A mean the surest lot,
That lies too high for base contempt,
  Too low for envy's shot.

My wishes are but few,
  All easy to fulfil;
I make the limits of my power
  The bonds unto my will.

I have no hopes but one,
  Which is of heavenly reign;
Effects attained, or not desired,
  All lower hopes refrain.

14. "Silly" meaning *simple*.

I feel no care of coin;
  Well-doing is my wealth
My mind to me an empire is,
  While grace affordeth health.

I clip high-climbing thoughts,
  The wings of swelling pride;
Their fall is worst, that from the height
  Of greatest honors slide.

Since sails of largest size
  The storm doth soonest tear,
I bear so low and small a sail
  As freeth me from fear.

I wrestle not with rage,
  While fury's flame doth burn;
It is in vain to stop the stream
  Until the tide doth turn.

But when the flame is out,
  And ebbing wrath doth end,
I turn a late enraged foe
  Into a quiet friend.

And taught with often proof,
  A tempered calm I find
To be most solace to itself,
  Best cure for angry mind.

Spare diet is my fare,
  My clothes more fit than fine;
I know I feed and clothe a foe
  That pampered would repine.

I envy not their hap,
  Whom favor doth advance;
I take no pleasure in their pain,
  That have less happy chance.

To rise by other's fall
  I deem a losing gain;
All states with others' ruins built
  To ruin run amain.[15]

No change of Fortune's calms
  Can cast my comforts down;
When Fortune smiles, I smile to think
  How quickly she will frown.

And when in froward mood
  She proves an angry foe,
Small gain I found to let her come,
  Less loss to let her go.

15. "Amain," meaning *with full force.*

BLESSED JOHN THULIS

(1568–MARCH 18, 1616)

JOHN THULIS WAS BORN in Upholland, a small town in Lancashire, around 1568. A deeply traditional region, Lancashire was the home of many recusants and Catholic sympathizers. Like much of Northern England, Lancashire was well-represented in the rebellions against Henry VIII's reforms, including the 1536 Pilgrimage of Grace, a popular uprising in protest of liturgical changes and the dissolution of the monasteries. In the 1560s, Lancashire played a role in the Northern Rebellion, in which Catholic nobles rose against Elizabeth. Thus, while very little is known about Thulis's family or early education, his ardent Catholicism is not entirely surprising, given his birthplace.

In 1583, a year and a half after the sensational and highly publicized trial and execution of the Jesuit Edmund Campion, the fifteen-year-old Thulis left England to study at the English College in Rheims. He studied there until he was sent to Rome for his ordination in 1590, and subsequently prepared to join the English mission. He arrived in England in early 1592, to find the English government agitated by fears of Catholic invasion and rebellion and on a determined hunt for priests. Thulis was quickly captured and imprisoned with other priests at Wisbech Castle, where it seems he remained a prisoner for several years. Somehow, however, he escaped and continued in his pastoral mission, heading back to his home county of Lancashire. He evaded further capture for many years, hiding with Catholic families and administering sacraments, but he was finally caught again in either 1615 or 1616, and held in the formidable Lancaster Castle along with other priests and Catholic non-conformists.

In Lancaster Castle, John Thulis was imprisoned with a weaver named Roger Wrenno, a zealous Catholic layman who would ultimately join Thulis in martyrdom. One evening in 1616, shortly before they were brought to trial, Thulis and Wrenno somehow managed to escape the castle, and walked vigorously all through the night. When the sun rose, however, they found that they had walked in a large circle and were in the immediate vicinity of Lancaster Castle. They were re-apprehended, and Thulis was placed in a cell with some thieves, four of whom he converted, and three of whom would be executed alongside him.

Thulis and his companions were quickly brought to trial, and he was accused of treason and practicing as a Catholic priest, while Wrenno was on trial for the felony of harboring and assisting priests. A contemporary anonymous poem written to celebrate the martyrdoms of Thulis and Wrenno mentions that the court brought a famed preacher to interrogate Thulis, and to "try his constancy," but that Thulis answered all questions cheerfully and meekly. Another account records that one of the judges at the trial was so moved by Thulis's manner that he praised the prisoner for his modesty, prudence, and temper. Thulis was offered clemency and release if he would take an oath affirming allegiance to the King as head of the Church of England, but Thulis consistently refused, and was condemned to death.

The poem, "The Song of a Happy Rising," was composed during these last days, and probably left with other priests in the prison when he was taken out to execution. In the manuscript source, the poem is introduced as being "The Song Which Mr. Thulis Writ For Himself," and we can imagine the poet using the poem as a means of meditation, prayer, and consolation in the face of death. The song, however, also has elements of exhortation, and the poet is certainly writing to and for others. In the first stanza, for instance, we can see Thulis' rich charity in his concern for those who might be saddened by his execution, that they may "cease to lament" (ln. 1) and have firm faith in Christ and a "joyful rising" (ln. 8). Indeed, it is this firm hope in the Resurrection that consistently triumphs over death throughout the poem, and the refrain of a happy or joyful rising with Christ at the end of each stanza consoles and redirects the reader's attention from death to joyful life.

Thulis was executed on March 18, 1616. Although he was offered a final chance to take the oath while on the scaffold, he once again refused. An anonymous poem giving an account of his execution records that he was charitable and forgiving to his executioners and those pleading with him to take the oath, and that when his body was cut into pieces, the crowds watching the scene soaked their handkerchiefs in his blood to preserve as relics, a suggestive detail about the religious sympathies of the people he had come back to serve in Lancashire. His body was quartered and sent to four of the prominent towns of the county: Lancaster, Preston, Wiggan, and Warrington. In Preston, his severed limbs were attached to the church steeple, and his head was mounted on the walls of Lancaster Castle.

Thulis's companion Roger Wrenno was hung immediately after Thulis, but the rope broke before he died, and he fell to the ground. When he dazedly recovered consciousness, the authorities once again offered him his life in exchange for the oath of allegiance. But Wrenno jumped up and ran back up the scaffold, saying he was of the same mind as before. When the Sheriff asked him why he was in such haste, Wrenno replied, "O! If you had seen what I have just now seen, you would be as much in haste to die as I now am."

Sources and Further Reading

Gradwell, Robert. *Venerable John Thules: The Upholland Martyr.* London: Catholic Truth Society, 1896.

Pollen, John Hungerford, S.J. "Chapter X: Venerable John Thulis and Venerable Roger Wrenno." In *Acts of English Martyrs,* pp. 194–207. London: Burns and Oates, 1891.

The Poetry of Blessed John Thulis

‡ ‡ ‡

The Song of a Happy Rising

True Christian hearts cease to lament,
For grief it is in vain,
For Christ you know was well content
To suffer bitter pain
That we may come to heaven's bliss,
There joyfully to sing.
Who doth believe shall never miss
To have a joyful rising!

But, England, hear. My heart is sad
For thy great cruelty
And loss of faith which once thou had
Of Christianity.
In thee false doctrine doth appear
Abundantly to spring,
Which is the cause, I greatly fear,
Thou lose thy happy rising!

As for myself, I am not afraid
To suffer constantly,
For why? Due debt must need be paid
Unto sweet God on high.
Saint Paul, he being firm of faith,
Hoping with saints to sing,
Most patiently did suffer death.
Lord, send us happy rising!

Mark well my ghostly victory,
  My friends both great and small;
Be firm of faith, remember me
  And dread not of your fall;
For you, my sheep, I shepherd have
  Made labor for to bring
You to my fold, your souls to save.
  Christ, send us happy rising!

I have said Mass and Matins both
  And true Instructions taught,
Confirmed by the Holy Ghost
  And mighty power wrought;
The Holy Communion also
  With manna ever living,
The Holy Sacraments I taught.
  Lord, send us happy rising!

Christ's passion oft before your face
  I have declared plain,
How for our sins he suffered death
  And how he rose again;
And how the twelve Apostles eke
  Were put to death for preaching
The Catholic faith which Christ did teach.
  Christ, send us happy rising!

St. Andrew, he condemned was
  Upon a cross to die.
They could not hurt his sacred soul,
  She to thee then did fly.
There stretched forth her arms so wide
  Most joyfully did sing,

That we with her may there abide,
  Christ send us happy rising.

St. James he never did refuse
  Most faithfully to pray;
Even when the cruel-hearted Jews
  Did take his life away.
And St. Bartholomew also,
  Alive did lose his skin;
Yea, for his truth and confidence
  In Christ our heavenly King.

St. John Evangelist did preach,
  Being simply arrayed,
The Catholic faith in England here
  Though now it be decayed.
St. James the more, 'headed was he
  Of death he felt the sting,
Although he lived virtuously,
  Lord send us happy rising.

St. Matthew lost his life because
  God's word he did maintain;
And many saints in like case
  Which truth could not refrain.
St. Thomas, the Apostle, clear,
  He, by a cruel king,
Was murdered with a hateful spear,
  Lord, send us happy rising.

St. Paul, a Catholic of Rome
  For love of Christ he bear,
Did lose his life, but yet his fame
  Is spread both far and near.

St. Stephen was stoned to death also
  And when he lay a-dying,
He prayed for his enemies,
  Christ send us happy rising.

Moreover, Mark Evangelist,
  A cruel death died he:
A rope about his neck was cast
  And dragged to death was he.
St. Lawrence on a grid-iron hot
  Did lie most freshly frying
Was put to cruel death, God wot,[1]
  Christ send us happy rising.

And many saints and martyrs mo'e-
  Which were too long to write,
Have suffered cruel death you know,
  As scripture doth recite.
They now with Christ above do reign
  And joyfully do sing,
That we may all God's love attain,
  Christ send us happy rising.

And then why should I be afraid
  To suffer constantly,
Since in this case so many saints
  Did suffer patiently
And left examples for us all
  That we with them may sing,
God grant we may for mercy call
  And have a happy rising.

1. "Wot," meaning *knows*.

Oh you poor prisoners, dread not death,
  Though you have done amiss.
But pray to God with faithful hearts
  To bring you into bliss.
Confess your sins with contrite hearts
  Unto your heavenly King,
For he is merciful indeed:
  Christ send us happy rising.

There is no man lives in such case
  That hath not done amiss;
Yet through repentance and God's grace,
  May reap eternal bliss.
Our Savior there did suffer death
  Poor souls in bliss to bring
Unto that blessed heavenly place,
  God send us joyful rising.

The saints also did suffer death,
  And martyrs, as you hear,
And I myself am now at hand,
  And death I do not fear.
Then have I trust of greater grace
  Unto my soul will bring,
When we shall meet both face to face
  Before our heavenly King.

No hurdle hard nor hempen rope
  Can make me once afraid,
No tyrant's knife against my life
  Shall make me dismayed.
Though flesh and bones be broken and torn.
  My soul I trust will sing

Amongst the glorious company
  With Christ our heavenly King.

Thus I your friend John Thulis,
  Have made my latest end,
Desiring God when his will is
  Us all to heaven send,
Where neither strange nor damned crew
  Can grief unto us bring,
And now I bid my last adieu.
  Christ, send us happy rising!

God grant you grace still in your hearts
  False doctrine to refrain
And hold the true Catholic faith
  Which Christ did once ordain.
All honor be to God of hosts,
  All glory to his Son,
All praise be to the Holy Ghost,
  Three Persons all in One.

BLESSED NICHOLAS POSTGATE, D.D.

(1596–AUGUST 7, 1679)

NICHOLAS POSTGATE HAS the unusual distinction of receiving martyrdom at the ripe age of eighty-three. No less remarkable, in fact, is that Postgate had worked clandestinely as a Catholic priest for forty-nine years before being caught. In contrast, Edmund Campion was apprehended barely more than a year after his landing on English soil as a priest; Robert Southwell was comparatively long-lasting, evading capture for six years. Postgate's forty-nine years, in this context, is incredible, and the salutary effects of such a lengthy ministry are easy to imagine. Indeed, in a letter that Postgate sent to a friend at Douai after thirty-four years in England, he writes that he had reconciled twenty-four hundred lapsed Catholics to Church, buried seven hundred and nineteen with Catholic rites, baptized five hundred and ninety-three infants, and married two hundred and twenty-six couples. Furthermore, he mentions six hundred current penitents, who regularly came to him for confession and absolution. Such activity had concrete consequences. By 1676, just three years before his execution, the Catholic population in the northern English communities which he served had grown so extensively that more than a third of all adults were professing the Catholic faith.

Nicholas Postgate's parents were Yorkshire farmers, known recusants who had been reported to the authorities and heavily fined for marrying and baptizing their children in secret—a sign that, rather than attend the Anglican Church, they were seeking out hidden Catholic priests for the sacraments. He was born in 1596, and his father died in 1602, leaving his mother Margaret to raise and educate Nicholas and his two brothers alone. In 1621, he left England and entered the English College at Douai. Ordained in 1628, he returned to England two years later, at the age of thirty-four, and spent the many years left to him serving the Catholics in his native region. For some years, he was attached to the households of various Catholic gentry, but by the 1660s, he had moved into a small farmhouse in the moors of North Yorkshire, and worked from there, quietly ministering to the surrounding Catholics. To signal that he was at home, he would hang some sheets over a hedge, as if to air them out, and he would use a similar system when he visited other farms or wanted to indicate the location and time of mass. Tradition also records that he loved flowers, and in some accounts he was the first to bring daffodils to the moors, planting and cultivating them in his own gardens.

Charles II, who had taken the throne in 1660 after the English Civil War and the Interregnum, was more inclined towards religious tolerance than some of his predecessors, and active persecutions against Catholics had softened, although it was still technically illegal to help priests, and treasonous to be one. In 1678, however, a man named Titus Oates fabricated a monstrous plot in which, he claimed, Catholics aimed to assassinate Charles II and install a Catholic monarch. Calling it the "Popish Plot," Oates riled up fears to a nearly hysterical pitch, and instigated fierce new persecutions against Catholics throughout England. Although many innocents were executed, it eventually became clear that Oates had invented the Plot, and he was tried and convicted for perjury by the English government. In the height of these persecutions, Postgate was finally caught, arrested while performing a baptism in a rural hamlet. The father of the baptized child, Matthew Lyth, was taken into custody with two other yeomen who were present. Lyth refused to speak anything against Postgate, however, and was imprisoned and interrogated for months, not being released until after Postgate's execution.

In Postgate's trial, he was found guilty of being a priest, and sentenced the traitor's death of hanging, drawing, and quartering, despite his arguments that he had no political aims and was merely serving the spiritual needs of English Catholics. In prison following his conviction, he was visited by a woman who had testified against him in the trial, and he forgave her and gave her his blessing. By all accounts, he was in high spirits, and spent his time in prison singing and composing hymns; it is thought that the hymn included here dates from this period. On August 7, 1679, he was executed, and his reported last words were:

> I die in the Catholic religion, out of which there is no salvation; Mr. Sheriff, you know I die not for the Plot, but for my religion. I pray God bless the King and the royal family. Be pleased, Mr. Sheriff, to acquaint his Majesty, that I never offended him in any manner of way. I pray God give him his grace, and the light of truth. I forgive all that have wronged me, and brought me to this death, and I desire forgiveness of all people.

Nicholas Postgate's quartered body was venerated by the many Catholics in the surrounding communities, and many of his relics are still preserved and honored in parishes throughout Yorkshire. His hymn became widely popular, and he came to be commonly known as the "priest of the moors" or the "martyr of the moors." To this day, the Diocese of Middlesbrough holds an annual "Postgate Rally" on the first Sunday of July, which includes mass and veneration of his relics. The rally concludes each year with the singing of Postgate's hymn.

Sources and Further Reading

Hamilton, Elizabeth. *The Priest of the Moors: Reflections on Nicholas Postgate*. London: Darton, Longman & Todd, 1980.

M. M. M. "Venerable Nicholas Postgate, Martyr." *The Life of the Spirit*, Vol. 2, No. 18 (August 1945): pp. 102–107.

Sheils, William Joseph. "Postgate, Nicholas (c. 1596–1679)." In *Oxford Dictionary of National Biography*. New York: Oxford University Press, 2004.

The Poetry of Blessed Nicholas Postgate, D.D.

‡ ‡ ‡

Postgate's Hymn

Oh gracious God, Oh Savior sweet,
 Oh Jesus, think on me,
And suffer me to kiss thy feet,
 Though late I come to thee.

Behold, dear Lord, I come to thee
 With sorrow and with shame,
For when thy bitter wounds I see,
 I know I cause the same.

Sweet Jesus, who shall lend me wings
 Of peace and perfect love,
That I may rise from earthly things
 To rest with thee above?

For sin and sorrow overflow
 All earthly things so high,
That I can find no rest below,
 But unto thee I fly.

Wherefore my soul doth loathe the things
 Which gave it once delight,
And unto thee, the King of Kings,
 Would mount with all her might.

And yet the weight of flesh and blood
 Doth so my wings restrain,

That oft I strive and gain no good,
  But rise, to fall again.

Yet when this fleshly misery
  Is master'd by the mind,
I cry "Avaunt all vanity,"
  And "Satan, stand behind."

So thus, sweet Lord, I fly about
  In weak and weary case
Like the lone dove which Noah sent out
  And found no resting place.

My weary wings, sweet Jesu, mark,
  And when thou thinkest best
Stretch forth thy arm from out the ark,
  And take me to thy rest. Amen.

Another Version of the Same Hymn

Blessed God, Oh Savior sweet,
  Oh Jesus, look on me!
Oh Christ, my King, refuse me not,
  Though late I come to thee!

I come to thee, confounded quite
  With sorrow and with shame,
When I beheld thy bitter wounds
  And knew I did the same.

I am the wretch that crowned thee,
  I made those wounds so wide;
I nailed thee unto the cross,
  With spear I pierced thy side.

Thy side, thy belly eke,[1] I rent
  With whip and cruel rod,
'Twas I that wrought thee all that woe,
  Forgive me, my good God.

For only pride of cherubim,
  How many thousands fell
From pleasure to perpetual pain,
  From heaven to hateful hell.

More than a thousand thousand times
  Have I deserved thine ire:
Yet do I, myself, still remain
  And feel not yet hell-fire.

---

1. "Eke," meaning *also*.

Yet do I still thy favor find,
  Yet thou dost keep me still
Against the force of all my foes
  That seek my soul to spill.

Yet more than this, that I might live,
  Thou diedst on the rood;
And to redeem my soul from hell,
  Thou spent thy dearest blood.

That precious blood, which from thy side
  Came gushing out amain,[2]
Was spent to save my sinful soul
  From endless woe and pain.

Alas! my Lord, most merciful,
  What have I done or wrought,
That thou shouldst like so well of me?
  What have I said or thought?

What didst thou see in me, vile wretch?
  Oh God, what didst thou see?
What moved thee, Oh Judge most just,
  To take such ruth[3] of me?

Oh come angels, come archangels,
  Come saints and souls divine;
Come martyrs and confessors, eke,
  Your aid to me assign.

2. "Amain," meaning *with full force.*
3. "Ruth," meaning *compassion* or *pity.*

Lend me your help, your counsel give,
  Oh tell me how I may
Relieve my Lord that loves me so,
  Which am but dust and clay.

All worldly honor now farewell,
  All wicked wealth adieu;
Pride and vain-glory pack you hence,
  Too long I served you.

In you I dreamed my joy had been,
  But I deceived was;
And now broad-waking I do see
  That it hangs on the cross.

Upon the cross, between two thieves,
  Stark dead, alack! he hangs.
For me, the child of endless death,
  He felt the bitter pangs.

Oh that it once were my good chance
  To kiss those wounds so wide;
Oh that my heart had once the hap,
  To harbor in his side.

Oh that I might with Magdalene,
  Embrace his fastened feet,
Or with the good thief hang by him,
  A thing for me more meet.

Then would I boldly dare to say
  That neither rack nor cord,
Nor any torments in the world
  Debar me from my Lord.

Then Machavell, with all his sleights,
Should not once make me moan;
No Turk, nor tyrant, no, nor devil,
Should make me leave my Lord.

Grant, blessed God, grant Savior sweet,
Grant, Jesus, King of Bliss,
That in thy love I live and die,
Sweet Jesus, grant me this.

APPENDIX

THIS APPENDIX IS INTENDED as a supplement to the selection of poems included in the original edition of *Lyra Martyrum*. It includes an epistle and several more poems by Robert Southwell, as well as poems by English Catholics who, though not martyrs, nevertheless suffered considerably for their faith.

ROBERT SOUTHWELL[1]

[Prefatory Epistle]

Poets, by abusing their talent, and making the follies and feignings of love the customary subject of their base endeavors, have so discredited this faculty that a poet, a lover, and a liar are by many reckoned but three words of one signification. But the vanity of men cannot counterpease the authority of God, who delivering many parts of scripture in verse, and by his apostle willing us to exercise our devotion in hymns and spiritual sonnets, warranteth the art to be good and the use allowable. And therefore not only among the heathens whose gods were chiefly canonized by their poets, and their paynim divinity oracled in verse, but even in the Old and New Testament, it hath been used by men of greatest piety in matters of most devotion. Christ himself, by making a hymn the conclusion of his last supper and the prologue to the first pageant of his passion, gave his spouse a method to imitate, as in the office of the Church it appeareth, and all men a pattern to know the true use of this measured and footed style. But the Devil, as he affecteth deity, and seeketh to have all the complements of divine honor applied to his service, so hath he among the rest possessed also most poets with his idle fancies. For in lieu of solemn and devout matter, to which in duty they owe their abilities, they now busy themselves in expressing such passions as only serve for testimonies to how unworthy affections they have wedded their wills. And because the best course to let them see the error of their works is to weave a new web in their own loom, I have here laid a few coarse threads together to invite some skillfuller wits to go forward in the same, or to begin some finer piece wherin it may be seen how well verse and virtue suite together. Blame me not (good cousin) though I send you a blameworthy present, in which the most that can commend it is the goodwill of the writer, neither art nor invention giving it any credit. If in me this be a fault, you cannot be faultless that did importune me to commit it, and therefore you must bear part of the penance, when it shall please sharp censures to impose. In the meantime, with many good wishes I send you these few ditties; add you the tunes and let the mean, I pray you, be still a part in all your music.

1. For the following Southwell letter and poems, the source text that has been modernized here is in the aforementioned St. Robert Southwell, *Collected Poems*.

‡ ‡ ‡

Saint Peter's Complaint

How can I live, that have my life denied?
What can I hope, that lost my hope in fear?
What trust to one that truth itself defied?
What good in him, that did his God forswear?
  Oh sin of sins, of evils the very worst,
  Oh sinful wretch of sinners most accurst.

I vaunted erst though all his friends had failed,
Alone with Christ all fortunes to have tried,
And lo I craved first of all was quailed,
Excelling none but in untruth and pride.
  Such distance is between high words and deeds;
  In proof the greatest vaunter seldom speeds.

If tyrant's bloody threats had me dismayed,
Or smart of cruel torments made me yield,
There had been some pretense to be afraid.
I should have fought before I lost the field,
  But, Oh!, infamous foil of maiden's breath
  Did blow me down and blast my soul to death.

Was I to stay the Church, a chosen rock,
That with so soft a gale was overthrown?
Was I chief pastor of the faithful flock,
To guide their souls, that murdered thus my own?
  A rock of ruin, not a rest to stay,
  A pastor not to feed but to betray.

Could servile fear of rendering nature's due,
Which growth in years was shortly like to claim.

So thrall my love that I should thus eschew
A vowed death and miss so fair an aim?
  Die, die disloyal wretch, thy life detest
  For saving thine, thou hast forsworn the best.

Was life so dear and Christ become so base
I of so great, God of so small account,
That Peter needs must follow Judas' race
And all the Jews in cruelty surmount?
  And yet Judas deemed thirty pence his price;
  I worse than he for naught denied him thrice.

Where was the heart that did so little fear
The armed troops that him did apprehend?
Where was the sword that stroke off Malchus' ear?
Where was the faith of Christ's professed friend?
  Oh Adam's child, it was a silly Eve
  That thee of faith and force did thus bereave.

I, once designed judge to loose and bind,
Now plead at mercy's bar as guilty thrall;
Dove's son was once to me for name assigned,
My stony name now better suits my fall.
  My oaths were stones, my cruel tongue the sling
  My God the mark at which my spite did fling.

Were all the Jewish tyrannies too few
To glut thy hungry looks with his disgrace,
That thou more malice than they all must shew
And spit thy poison in thy maker's face?
  Didst thou to spare his foes put up thy sword,
  To brandish now thy tongue against thy lord?

Is this thy best deserving master's meed?
Is this the wage he earned with all his toil?
And didst thou vow thy help at every need,
Thus at the first encounter to recoil?
  Oh impious tongue, no tongue but viper's sting,
  That could with cursing oaths forswear thy king.

Oh tongue, the first that did his godhead sound,
How couldst thou utter such detesting words,
That every word was to his heart a wound
And lanced him deeper than a thousand swords?
  What Jewish race, yea what infernal sprite
  Could have disgorged against him greater spite?

With mercy, Jesu, measure my offence;
Let deep remorse thy due revenge abate;
Let tears appease when trespass doth incense;
Let mildness temper thy deserved hate;
  Let grace forgive, let love forget my fall;
  With fear I crave, with hope I humbly call.

Decease Release
DUM MORIOR ORIOR[2]

The pounded spice both taste and scent doth please;
In fading smoke the force doth incense show;
The perisht kernel springeth with increase;
The lopped tree doth best and soonest grow.

God's spice I was, and pounding was my due;
In fading breath my incense favored best;
Death was the mean my kernel to renew;
By lopping shot I up to heavenly rest.

Some things more perfect are in their decay,
Like spark that going out gives clearest light:
Such was my hap, whose doleful dying day
Began my joy and termed fortune's spite.

Alive a Queen, now dead I am a saint;
Once Mary called, my name now Martyr is;
From earthly reign debarred by restraint,
In lieu whereof I reign in heavenly bliss.

My life, my grief, my death, hath wrought my joy;
My friends, my foil, my foes, my weal procured,
My speedy death hath scorned long annoy,
And loss of life an endless life assured.

My scaffold was the bed where ease I found,
The block a pillow of eternal rest,

2. "While I die, I am being born."

My headman cast me in a blissful swound,[3]
His axe cut of my cares from cumbered breast.

Rue not my death, rejoice at my repose;
It was no death to me but to my woe,
The bud was opened to let out the rose,
The chains unloosed to let the captive go.

A prince by birth, a prisoner by mishap,
From crown to cross, from throne to thrall I fell.
My right my ruth, my titles wrought my trap;
My weal my woe, my worldly heaven my hell.

By death from prisoner to a prince enhanced;
From cross to crown, from thrall to throne again,
My ruth my right, my trap my style advanced
From woe to weal, from hell to heavenly reign.

3. "Swound," meaning *fainting fit.*

Love's Servile Lot

Love mistress is of many minds,
Yet few know whom they serve;
They reckon least how little Love
Their service doth deserve.

The will she robbeth from the wit,
The sense from reason's lore;
She is delightful in the rind,
Corrupted in the core.

She shroudeth vice in virtue's veil,
Pretending good in ill;
She offereth joy, affordeth grief,
A kiss where she doth kill.

A honey-shower rains from her lips,
Sweet lights shine in her face;
She hath the blush of virgin mind,
The mind of viper's race.

She makes thee seek, yet fear to find,
To find, but not enjoy;
In many frowns some gliding smiles
She yields to more annoy.

She woos thee to come near her fire,
Yet doth she draw it from thee;
Far off she makes thy heart to fry,
And yet to freeze within thee.

She letteth fall some luring baits
For fools to gather up;

Too sweet, too sour, to every taste
  She tempereth her cup.

Soft souls she binds in tender twist,
  Small flies in spinner's web;
She sets afloat some luring streams,
  But makes them soon to ebb.

Her watery eyes have burning force;
  Her floods and flames conspire;
Tears kindle sparks, sobs fuel are,
  And sighs do blow her fire.

May never was the month of love,
  For May is full of flowers;
But rather April, wet by kind,
  For love is full of showers.

Like tyrant, cruel wounds she gives,
  Like surgeon, salve she lends;
But salve and sore have equal force,
  For death is both their ends.

With soothing words enthralled souls
  She chains in servile bands;
Her eye in silence hath a speech
  Which eye best understands.

Her little sweet hath many sours,
  Short hap immortal harms;
Her loving looks are murd'ring darts,
  Her song bewitching charms.

Like winter rose and summer ice,
  Her joys are still untimely;
Before her hope, behind remorse,
  Fair first, in fine unseemly.

Moods, passions, fancy's jealous fits
  Attend upon her train;
She yieldeth rest without repose,
  And heaven in hellish pain.

Her house is Sloth, her door Deceit,
  And slippery Hope her stairs;
Unbashful Boldness bids her guests,
  And every vice repairs.

Her diet is of such delights
  As please till they be past;
But then the poison kills the heart
  That did entice the taste.

Her sleep in sin doth end in wrath,
  Remorse rings her awake;
Death calls her up, Shame drives her out,
  Despairs her upshot make.

Plough not the seas, sow not the sands,
  Leave off your idle pain;
Seek other mistress for your minds,
  Love's service is in vain.

Lewd Love Is Loss

Misdeeming eye, that stoopest to the lure
Of mortal worths, not worth so worthy love;
All beauty's base, all graces are impure,
That do thy erring thoughts from God remove.
Sparks to the fire, the beams yield to the sun,
All grace to God, from whom all graces run.

If picture move, more should the pattern please;
No shadow can with shadowed thing compare,
And fairest shapes, whereon our loves do seize,
But silly[4] signs of God's high beauties are.
Go, starving sense, feed thou on earthly maste,[5]
True love in heaven seek thou thy sweet repast.

Glean not in barren soil these offal ears,
Since reap thou mayst whole harvests of delight;
Base joys with griefs, bad hopes do end in fears,
Lewd love with loss, evil peace with deadly fight.
God's love alone doth end with endless ease,
Whose joys in hope, whose hope concludes in peace.

Lett not the luring train of fancies trap,
Or gracious features, proofs of Nature's skill,
Lull Reason's force asleep in Error's lap,
Or draw thy wit to bent of wanton will.
The fairest flowers have not the sweetest smell;
A seeming heaven proves oft a damning hell.

4. "Silly," meaning *simple* or *innocent*.
5. "Maste," meaning the fruit of woodland trees.

Self-pleasing souls, that play with beauty's bait,
In shining shroud may swallow fatal hook;
Where eager sight on semblant fair doth wait,
A lock it proves, that first was but a look.
The fish with ease into the net doth glide,
But to get out the way is not so wide.

So long the fly doth dally with the flame,
Until his singed wings do force his fall;
So long the eye doth follow fancy's game,
Till love hath left the heart in heavy thrall.
Soon may the mind be cast in Cupid's jail,
But hard it is imprisoned thoughts to bail.

Oh loathe that love whose final aim is lust,
Moth of the mind, eclipse of reason's light;
The grave of grace, the mole of Nature's rust,
The wrack of wit, the wrong of every right.
In sum, an evil whose harms no tongue can tell;
In which to live is death, to die is hell.

CHIDIOCK TICHBORNE

(1558?–1586)

Tichborne's Lament[1]

My prime of youth is but a frost of cares.
    My feast of joy is but a dish of pain.
My crop of corn is but a field of tares[2]—
    And all my good is but vain hope of gain.
The day is gone, and yet I saw no sun.
And now I live, and now my life is done.

The spring is past, and yet it hath not sprung.
    The fruit is dead, and yet the leaves are green.
My youth is gone, and yet I am but young.
    I saw the world, and yet I was not seen.
My thread is cut, and yet it is not spun—
And now I live, and now my life is done.

I sought my death, and found it in my womb.
    I looked for life, and saw it was a shade.
I trod the earth, and knew it was my tomb.
    And now I die, and now I am but made.

The glass is full, and now my glass is run,
And now I live, and now my life is done.

1. The source text that has been modernized here is taken from Richard S. M. Hirsch, "The Works of Chidiock Tichborne," *English Literary Renaissance*, Vol. 16, No. 2 (1986): pp. 309–10.
2. "Tares," meaning *weeds*.

HENRY CONSTABLE

(1562–1613)

‡ ‡ ‡

To the Blessed Martyr: Mary Queen of Scotland[1]

[1]
I write of tears and blood, at one time shed,
From one sweet body and ten thousand eyes,
When as a Queen became a sacrifice
Like to a lamb unto a scaffold led.
Unworthy altar to be honored
With so dear off'ring of so high a price,
Whose loss no tears can show nor words suffice
The authors shame abroad the world to spread.
My ink even weeps, and tears with mourning black
Made ink again serve to record this lack,
And that dear blood which gushed from her face
Disdaining now upon the ground to bleed
To their face came, which caus'd this doleful case,
And made them blush for shame of such a deed.

[2]

It is not pomp of solemn funeral
That can excuse the crime those did commit,
Which after bloody sentence did permit
Thy sacred body to have burial.
Nor yet schism-rites can honor it at all;
Prophane they be, for such a corpse unfit;
Nature, which graced all her works, with it
Made all her marks to honor it withal.
The earth the chest, the heavens the hearse will be,
When night—the air with shadows covering
The sky—all hung with mourning black we see,
The stars as lights severe to adorn this hearse.
And now me thinks the angels dirges sing,
And stop my mouth and bid me end my verse.

[3]

I do thee wrong, Oh Queen, in that I say
The angels dirge sing to honor thee,
Since neither men nor angels use to pray
For such as die from sin's pollution free.
If any spot in innocence could be,
thy bloody baptism washed it away,
and that which seem'd thy funeral to me,
was made in heaven thy coronation day.
Then in the court, where God himself is king,
His mother Queen, and by whose princely side
For knights and dames, martyrs and virgins stand,
The angels thee unto God's throne did bring,

1. The source text for these three sonnets, which have been modernized here, is Maria Jesus Perez-Jauregui's "A Queen in a 'Purple Robe': Henry Constable's Poetic Tribute to Mary, Queen of Scots," in *Studies in Philology*, Vol. 113, No. 3 (2016): pp. 581–82.

Where, in the purple robe thy blood had died,
Thou took'st the crown of glory from his hand.

Spiritual Sonnets: To the Honor of God and His Saints[2]

To God the Father

Great God! within whose simple essence we
  Nothing but that which is thyself can find:
  When on thyself thou did'st reflect thy mind,
Thy thought was God, which took the form of thee.
And when this God, thus born, thou lov'st, and he
  Lov'd thee again with passion of like kind,
  (As lovers' sighs which meet become one wind)
Both breathed one Spright of equal deity.
Eternal Father! whence these two do come
  And wil'st the title of my father have,
  An heavenly knowledge in my mind engrave,
That it thy Son's true image may become;
And scent my heart with sighs of holy Love,
That it the temple of the Spright may prove.

To God the Son

Great Prince of heaven! begotten of that king,
  Who rules the kingdom that himself did make,
  And of that virgin Queen man's shape did take,
Which from King David's royal stock did spring:
No marvel though thy birth made angels sing,

2 The source text for these sonnets, which has been modernized here, is Thomas Park's *Heliconia: A Selection of English Poetry from the Elizabethan Age: Written or Published between 1575–1604*, vol. 2 (London: Longman, Hurst, Rees, Orme, and Brown, 1815).

And angels' ditties shepherd's pipes awake,
And kings like shepherds, humbled for thy sake,
Kneel at thy feet and gifts of homage bring:
For heaven and earth, the high and low estate,
As partners of thy birth make equal claim.
Angels, because in heaven God thee begat,
Shepherds and kings, because thy mother came
From princely race, and yet by poverty
Made glory shine in her humility.

To God the Holy Ghost

Eternal Spright! which art in heaven the love
With which God and his Son each other kiss,
And who, to show who God's beloved is,
The shape and wings took'st of a loving dove;
When Christ ascending sent thee from above
In fiery tongues, thou cam'st down unto his,
That skill in uttering heavenly mysteries,
By heat of zeal both faith and love might move.
True God of Love! from whom all true love springs,
Bestow upon my love thy wings and fire;
My soul a spirit is, and with thy wings
May like an angel fly from earth's desire:
And with thy fire a heart inflamed may bear,
And in thy sight a seraphim appear.

To the Blessed Sacrament

When thee, Oh holy sacrificèd Lamb,
In severed signs I white and liquid see,
As on thy body slain, I think on thee

Which pale by shedding of thy blood became.
And when again I do behold the same
  Veiled in white to be received of me,
  Thou seemest in thy syndon[3] wrapped to be
Like to a corpse, whose monument I am.
Buried in me, unto my soul appear
Prisoned in earth and banished from thy sight,
  Like our forefathers, who in Limbo were.
Clear thou my thoughts, as thou did'st give them light;
And as thou others freed from purging fire,
Quench in my heart the flames of bad desire.

To Our Blessed Lady

In that, Oh Queen of queens, thy birth was free
  From guilt, which others doth of grace bereave
  When in their mothers' womb they life receive,
God as his sole-borne daughter lovèd thee.
To match thee like thy birth's nobility,
  He thee his Spirit for thy spouse did leave:
  Of whom thou did'st his only Son conceive,
And so was linked to all the Trinity.
Cease then, Oh queens who earthly crowns do wear,
  To glory in the pomp of worldly things;
If men such high respect unto you bear
  Which daughters, wives, and mothers are of kings;
What honor should unto that Queen be done
Who had your God for father, spouse, and son?

3. "Syndon," meaning *shroud*.

To St. Michael the Archangel

When as the prince of angels, puffed with pride,
  Stirred his seditious spirits to rebel,
  God chose for chief his champion Michael,
And gave him charge the host of heaven to guide.
And when the angels of the rebels' side,
  Vanquished in battle, from their glory fell,
  The pride of heaven became the drake of hell,
And in the dungeon of despair was tied.
This dragon, since let loose, God's Church assailed,
And she, by help of Michael's sword, prevailed.
Who ever tried adventures like this knight,
  Which, general of heaven, hell overthrew,
For such a lady as God's spouse did fight,
  And such a monster as the devil subdue?

To St. John Baptist

As Anne, long barren, mother did become
  Of him, who last was judge in Israel;
  Thou, last of prophets borne, like Samuel
Did'st from a womb past hope of issue come.
His mother silent spake: "Thy father dumb
  Recovering speech, God's wonder did foretell."
  He, after death, a prophet was in hell,
And thou unborn within thy mother's womb.
He did anoint the king whom God did take
  From charge of sheep, to rule his chosen land.
But that high king who heaven and earth did make
  Received a holier liquor from thy hand,
When God his flock in human shape did feed,
As Israel's king kept his in shepherd's weed.

To St. Peter and St. Paul

He that for fear his master did deny,
  And at a maiden's voice amazèd stood,
  The mightiest monarch of the earth withstood,
And on his master's cross rejoiced to die.
He whose blind zeal did rage with cruelty,
  And helped to shed the first of martyr's blood,
  By light from heaven his blindness understood
And with the chief apostle slain doth lie.
Oh three times happy two! Oh golden pair,
  Who with your blood did lay the Church's ground
  Within the fatal town which twins did found.
And settled there the Hebrew fisher's chair,
Where first the Latin shepherd raised his throne,
And, since, the world and Church were ruled by one.

To St. Mary Magdalen

For few nights' solace in delicious bed,
  Where heat of lust did kindle flames of hell,
  Thou nak'd on naked rock in desert cell
Lay thirty years, and tears of grief did shed.
But for that time thy heart there sorrowed;
  Thou now in heaven eternally dost dwell,
  And for each tear, which from thine eyes then fell,
A sea of pleasure now is rendered.
If short delights entice my heart to stray,
  Let me by thy long penance learn to know
How dear I should for trifling pleasures pay,
  And if I virtue's rough beginning shun,
Let thy eternal joys unto me show
What high reward by little pain is won.

To St. Katherine

Because thou wast the daughter of a king,
  Whose beauty did all nature's works exceed,
  And wisdom, wonder to the world did breed,
A Muse might rouse itself on Cupid's wing.
But since these graces which from nature spring,
  Were grac'd by those which from grace did proceed,
  And glory hath deserved, my Muse doth need
An angel's feathers when thy praise I sing.
For all in thee became angelical:
  An angel's face had angel's purity,
And thou an angel's tongue did'st speak withal.
Loe, why thy soul, set free by martyrdom,
  Was crowned by God in angels' company,
And angels' hands thy body did entomb.

To St. Margaret

Fair Amazon of heaven! who took'st in hand
  Saint Michael and Saint George to imitate,
  And for a tyrant's love transformed to hate,
Wast for thy lily faith retained in band;
Alone, on foot, and with thy naked hand
  Thou did'st, like Michael and his host, and that
  For which on horse armed George we celebrate:
Whilst thou, like them, a dragon did'st withstand.
Behold my soul, shut in my body's jail,
  The which the drake of hell gapes to devour;
Teach me, Oh virgin! how thou did'st prevail?—
Virginity, thou sayest, was all thy aid.
  Give me then purity instead of power,
And let my soul, made chaste, pass for a maid.

To Our Blessed Lady

Sovereign of Queens! If vain ambition move
  My heart to seek an earthly prince's grace,
  Show me thy Son in his imperial place,
Whose servants reign our kings and queens above.
And if alluring passions I do prove,
  By pleasing sighs—show me thy lovely face,
  Whose beams the angels' beauty do deface,
And even inflame the seraphims with love.
So by ambition I shall humble be,
  When in the presence of the highest King
I serve all his, that he may honor me.
And Love, my heart to chaste desires shall bring,
  When fairest Queen looks on me from her throne,
And, jealous, bids me love but her alone.

To Our Blessed Lady

Why should I any love, Oh queen, but thee,
  If favor past a thankful love should breed?
  Thy womb did bear, thy breast my savior feed,
And thou did'st never cease to succor me.
If love do follow worth and dignity,
    Thou all in thy perfections dost exceed;
    If love be led by hope of future meed,
What pleasure more than thee in heaven to see?
An earthly sight doth only please the eye,
  And breeds desire, but doth not satisfy;
Thy sight gives us possession of all joy,
  And with such full delights each sense shall fill,
  As heart shall wish but for to see thee still,
And ever seeing, ever shall enjoy.

To Our Blessed Lady

Sweet Queen! although thy beauty raise up me
From sight of baser beauties here below,
Yet let me not rest there, but higher go
To him who took his shape from God and thee.
And if thy form in him more fair I see,
What pleasure from his deity shall flow,
By whose fair beams his beauty shineth so,
When I shall it behold eternally.
Then shall my love of pleasure have his fill,
When beauty's self in whom all pleasure is,
Shall my enamored soul embrace and kiss,
And shall new loves and new delights distill,
Which from my soul shall gush into my heart,
And through my body flow to every part.

To St. Mary Magdalen

Blessed offender! who thyself hast tried
How far a sinner differs from a saint,
Join thy wet eyes with tears of my complaint,
While I sigh for that grave for which thou cried.
No longer let my sinful soul abide
In fever of thy first desires faint,
But let that love which last thy heart did taint
With pangs of thy repentance pierce my side.
So shall my soul no foolish virgin be
With empty lamp; but like a Magdalen, bear
For ointment box a breast with oil of grace;
And so the zeal, which then shall burn in me,
May make my heart like to a lamp appear
And in my spouse's palace give me place.

To St. Mary Magdalen

Such as retired from sight of men, like thee,
By penance seek the joys of heaven to win,
In deserts make their paradise begin,
And even among wild beasts do angels see.
In such a place my soul doth seem to be
When in my body she laments her sin,
And none but brutal passions finds therein,
Except they be sent down from heaven to me.
Yet if those graces God to me impart,
Which he inspired thy blessed breast withal,
I may find heaven in my retired heart;
And if thou change the object of my love,
The winged affection which men Cupid call,
May get his sight, and like an angel prove.

HENRY VAUX[1]

(1559–1587)

‡ ‡ ‡

A Lamentation of a Sinner

Oh sovereign salve for sin,
        Which dost my soul behold,
That seeks herself from tangling faults
        By striving to unfold:
What plea shall I put in,
        When thou dost summons send,
To judge the people of the earth,
        And give the world an end;
When every deed and word,
        And every secret thought,
In open view of all the world
        Shall unto light be brought?

So many judges shall
        Against me sentence give,
As by example of good works
        Have taught how I should live.
So many pleaders shall

Confound my careful case,
As have in me by sound advice
Sought to increase thy grace.
So many shall that time
Against me witness bear,
As have beheld my fruitless faith,
And saw my sins appear.

Whereon whiles I do muse
In my amazed mind,
Forewarned through familiar foes,
Most fierce assaults I find.
My conscience to my face
Doth flatly me accuse;
My secret thoughts within my ears
Do whisper still these news;
Mine avarice doth bribe,
My pride doth brag me down;
Mine envy frets me like a file
At other folks' renown.

Concupiscence inflames,
And lust my limbs infects,
My meat doth burden, and my drink
My weakness great detects;
My slanders rent my fame,
Ambition doth supplant;
My greediness is not content,

1. For the following Vaux poems, the source text that has been modernized here is in Timothy Christopher Hacksley's "A Critical Edition of the Poems of Henry Vaux (c. 1559-1587) in MS. Folger BD with STC 22957" (Master's thesis, Rhodes University, 2008), pp. 7–18. Hacksley's excellent edition includes more of Vaux's poetry, helpful notes, and a facsimile of the manuscript.

But makes me wail for want;
My mirth but flattery is,
My sorrows are unkind;
My pleasures run me out of breath,
And griefs oppress my mind.

Behold, my God, whose might
May me a freeman make,
These were the friends, whose counsels cursed
I was content to take;
These were the lawless lords,
Whom I did serve alway;
These were the masters, whose mad hests
I did too much obey.
Behold my fall most foul,
Which folly first did frame;
In loving them I should have loath'd,
Whence breedeth all my blame.

Now do I look aloft
With hateful blushing face
On glory thine, that so I may
Discern mine own disgrace.
My many spots and great
Must needs increase my guilt,
Unless thou wash them in thy blood,
Which for my sake was spilt.
Forgive the faults, Oh Lord,
Which I from heart repent;
And grant my days to come may be
In thy sweet service spent.

In Hope, Patience

Despised things may live,
Although they pine in pain;
And things oft trodden under foot
May once yet rise again.

The stone which lies full low,
May be at last full high,
And stand on top of stately tower
In sight of every eye.

The roots of rotten reeds
In swelling seas are seen,
And when each tide hath tossed his worst,
They grow again full green.

I see no sight on earth
But it to change inclines;
And little clouds do overcast
The brightest sun that shines.

No flower is so fresh
But frost may it deface;
No man so sure in any seat,
But he may lose his place.

Wherefore I stand content,
Though much against my mind,
To take in worth this luckless lot
That is to me assigned.

No Trust in Fortune

Whoso doth trust the feigned cheer
That smileth forth by Fortune's looks,
When good to him she doth appear,
To take his life she layeth her hooks.

The mariner is most unwise
That trusteth to the quiet seas,
For commonly great storms arise
When as the winds so seem to cease.

Under the grass full fresh and green
There lurketh hid the hurtful snake;
Within the bait, as oft is seen,
Doth lie the hook, the fish to take.

To Fortune's wheel there is no trust,
For he that sits in highest place
Within an hour lieth in the dust,
If that she show a froward face.

Thus Fortune turneth uside down
Man's life, and changeth each estate;
She makes the poor man wear a crown,
The mighty prince she doth abate.

The wise man only 'scapeth free,
Nor subject is to Fortune's rage;
Though all estates her servants be,
Yet can she not subdue the sage.

Being Sick in Oxford thus He Prayed

With wailing voice from out the depth of sin,
To thee, Oh Lord, I silly wretch do cry,
Wherefore, Oh Lord, to hear me now begin;
Though death approach, let not thy servant die;
And though my ship be turned upside-down,
In seas of sin yet let me never drown.
As Jonah cried within the fish's maw,

Even so do I complain, now woeful wight;
As help from him thou didst not quite withdraw,
So let me find some mercy in thy sight;
And as thou cast him safe upon the land,
So out of sin, Lord, pull me with thy hand.

And as thou saved'st thy prophet in the cave
From greedy lions thirsting for their prey,
So from the ramping lion thou me save,
Which goeth about the silly souls to slay:
Though death and danger close me round about,
Yet know I, Lord, that thou canst bring me out.

Wherefore, Oh Lord, to thee I make my prayer;
Thou, Lord of Lords, vouchsafe to hear my voice;
Unto my griefs bow down thy piteous ear;
Though now I mourn, yet cause me to rejoice:
And grant me, Lord, to pass these seas of strife,
That I may come unto the port of life.

RICHARD CRASHAW

(1612–1613)

‡ ‡ ‡

FROM *Steps to the Temple*[1]

TO PONTIUS WASHING HIS HANDS

Thy hands are washed, but, oh, the water's spilt
That labored to have washed thy guilt;
The flood, if any can that can suffice,
Must have its fountain in thine eyes.

MARK 4

Why are ye afraid, Oh ye of little faith?

As if the storm meant him;
Or, 'cause heaven's face is dim,
    His needs a cloud.
Was ever froward wind
That could be so unkind,
    Or wave so proud?

The wind had need be angry, and the water black,
That, to the mighty Neptune's self, dare threaten wrack.

There is no storm but this
Of your own cowardice
That braves you out;
You are the storm that mocks
Your selves; you are the rocks
Of your own doubt:
Besides this fear of danger, there's no danger here,
And he that here fears danger, does deserve his fear.

UPON THE ASS THAT BORE OUR SAVIOR

Hath only anger an omnipotence
In eloquence?
Within the lips of love and joy doth dwell
No miracle?
Why else had Balaam's ass a tongue to chide
His masters pride?
And thou (heaven-burthen'd beast) hast ne're a word
To praise thy Lord?
That he should find a tongue and vocal thunder
Was a great wonder.
But oh me thinks 'tis a far greater one
That thou find'st none.

1. The source text that has been modernized here is taken from Richard Crashaw, *Steps to the Temple: Sacred Poems, with Other Delights of the Muses* (London: Printed by T. W. for Humphrey Moseley, 1646).

MATTHEW 27

And he answered them nothing

Oh mighty nothing! unto thee,
Nothing, we owe all things that be.
God spake once when he all things made,
He sav'd all when he nothing said.
The world was made of nothing then;
'Tis made by nothing now again.

SAINT MARY MAGDALENE, OR THE WEEPER[2]

Lo where a wounded heart with bleeding eyes conspire,
Is she a flaming fountain, or a weeping fire?

Hail, sister springs!
Parents of silver-footed rills!
Ever bubbling things!
Thawing crystal! snowy hills,
Still spending, never spent! I mean
Thy fair eyes, sweet Magdalene!

Heavens thy fair eyes be;
Heavens of ever-falling stars.
'Tis seed-time still with thee,
And stars thou sow'st, whose harvest dares
Promise the earth to counter-shine
Whatever makes heav'n's forehead fine.

But we're deceived all.
Stars indeed they are too true;
For they but seem to fall
As Heav'n's other spangles do.
It is not for our earth and us
To shine in things so precious.

Upwards thou dost weep.
Heav'n's bosom drinks the gentle stream;
Where th'milky rivers creep,
Thine floats above and is the cream.

2. The source text that has been modernized here is in Richard Crashaw's *Carmen Deo Nostro* (Paris: Peter Targa, 1652).

Waters above th'heavns, what they be
We're taught best by thy tears and thee.

Every morn from hence
A brisk cherub something sips
Whose sacred influence
Adds sweetness to his sweetest lips,
Then to his music. And his song
Tastes of this breakfast all day long.

Not in the evening's eyes
When they red with weeping are
For the sun that dies,
Sits sorrow with a face so fair,
Nowhere but here did ever meet
Sweetness so sad, sadness so sweet.

When sorrow would be seen
In her brightest majesty
(For she is a queen)
Then is she dressed by none but thee.
Then, and only then, she wears
Her proudest pearls; I mean, thy tears.

The dew no more will weep
The primrose's pale cheek to deck;
The dew no more will sleep
Nuzzel'd in the lily's neck;
Much rather would it be thy tear,
And leave them both to tremble here.

There's no need at all
That the balsam-sweating bough
So coyly should let fall

His med'cinable tears; for now
Nature hath learn't t'extract a dew
More sovereign and sweet from you.

Yet let the poor drops weep
(Weeping is the ease of woe)
Softly let them creep,
Sad that they are vanquished so.
They, though to others no relief,
Balsam may be, for their own grief.

Such the maiden gem[3]
By the purpling vine put on,
Peeps from her parent stem
And blushes at the bridegroom sun.
This watery blossom of thy eyn[4],
Ripe, will make the richer wine.

When some new bright guest
Takes up among the stars a room,
And Heav'n will make a feast,
Angels with crystal vials come
And draw from these full eyes of thine
Their master's water: their own wine.

Golden though he be,
Golden Tagus[5] murmurs though;
Were his way by thee,
Content and quiet he would go.

---

3. "Gem," meaning *flower.*
4. "Eyn," meaning *eyes.*
5. "Tagus," *a river in Spain and Portugal.*

So much more rich would he esteem
Thy silver than his golden stream.

Well does the May that lies
Smiling in thy cheeks, confess
The April in thine eyes.
Mutual sweetness they express.
No April e're lent kinder showers,
Nor May returned more faithful flowers.

Oh cheeks! Beds of chaste loves
By your own showers seasonably dashed.
Eyes! nests of milky doves
In your own wells decently washed.
Oh wit of love! that thus could place
Fountain and garden in one face.

Oh sweet contest: of woes
With loves, of tears with smiles disputing!
Oh fair, and friendly foes,
Each other kissing and confuting!
While rain and sunshine, cheeks and eyes
Close in kind contrarieties.

But can these fair floods be
Friends with the bosom fires that fill you!
Can so great flames agree
Eternal tears should thus distill thee?
Oh floods, oh fires! oh suns, oh showers!
Mixed and made friends by love's sweet powers.

'Twas his well-pointed dart
That digged these wells, and dressed this vine;
And taught the wounded heart

The way into these weeping eyn.
Vain loves avant! bold hands forbear!
The lamb hath dipped his white foot here.

And now where're he strays,
Among the Galilean mountains
Or more unwelcome ways,
He's followed by two faithful fountains;
Two walking baths; two weeping motions;
Portable and compendious oceans.

Oh Thou, thy lord's fair store!
In thy so rich and rare expenses,
Even when he showed most poor,
He might provoke the wealth of princes.
What prince's wanton'st pride e're could
Wash with silver, wipe with gold?

Who is that King, but he
Who calls't his crown to be called thine,
That thus can boast to be
Waited on by a wandering mine,
A voluntary mint, that strows
Warm silver showers where're he goes!

O precious prodigal!
Fair spendthrift of thyself! Thy measure
(Merciless love!) is all.
Even to the last pearle in thy treasure.
All places, times, and objects be
Thy tear's sweet opportunity.

Does the day-star rise?
Still thy stars do fall and fall.

Does day close his eyes?
Still the fountain weeps for all.
Let night or day do what they will,
Thou hast thy task; thou weepest still.

Does thy song lull the air?
Thy falling tears keep faithful time.
Does thy sweet-breath'd prayer
Up in clouds of incense climb?
Still at each sigh, that is, each stop,
A bead, that is, a tear, does drop.

At these thy weeping gates,
(Watching their wat'ry motion)
Each winged moment waits,
Takes his tear, and gets him gone.
By thine eye's tinct ennobled thus
Time lays him up; he 's precious.

Not, so long she lived,
Shall thy tomb report of thee;
But, so long she grieved,
Thus must we date thy memory.
Others by moments, months, and years
Measure their ages; thou, by tears.

So do perfumes expire,
So sigh tormented sweets, oppressed
With proud unpitying fires.
Such tears the suff'ring rose that's vexed
With ungentle flames does shed,
Sweating in a too warm bed.

Say, ye bright brothers,
The fugitive sons of those fair eyes
—Your fruitful mothers!—
What make you here? what hopes can 'tice
You to be born? what cause can borrow
You from those nests of noble sorrow?

Whither away so fast?
For sure the sordid earth
Your sweetness cannot taste
Nor does the dust deserve your birth.
Sweet, whither hast you then? Oh, say
Why you trip so fast away?

We go not to seek
The darlings of Aurora's bed,
The rose's modest cheek
Nor the violet's humble head,
Though the field's eyes too weepers be
Because they want such tears as we.

Much less mean we to trace
The fortune of inferior gems,
Preferred to some proud face
Or perched upon feared diadems.
Crowned heads are toys. We go to meet
A worthy object, our Lord's feet.

CLUNY MEDIA

Designed by Fiona Cecile Clarke, the CLUNY MEDIA *logo*
depicts a monk at work in the scriptorium,
with a cat sitting at his feet.

The monk represents our mission to emulate
the invaluable contributions of the monks
of Cluny in preserving the libraries of the West,
our strivings to know and love the truth.

The cat at the monk's feet is Pangur Bán, from the
eponymous Irish poem of the 9th century.
The anonymous poet compares his scholarly
pursuit of truth with the cat's happy hunting of mice.
The depiction of Pangur Bán is an homage to the work
of the monks of Irish monasteries and a sign
of the joy we at Cluny take in our trade.

"Messe ocus Pangur Bán,
cechtar nathar fria saindan:
bíth a menmasam fri seilgg,
mu memna céin im saincheirdd."

Made in the USA
Middletown, DE
08 March 2025

72345889R00154